MAJOR LEAGUE DADS

BASEBALL'S BEST PLAYERS REFLECT ON THE
FATHERS WHO INSPIRED THEM TO LOVE THE GAME

Kevin Neary and Leigh A. Tobin
Foreword by Terry Francona

RUNNING PRESS
PHILADELPHIA · LONDON

Published by Running Press,
A Member of the Perseus Books Group

Books published by Running Press are available at special discounts for bulk purchases in
the United States by corporations, institutions, and other organizations. For more informa-
tion, please contact the Special Markets Department at the Perseus Books Group, 2300
Chestnut Street, Suite 200, Philadelphia, PA 19103, or call (800) 810–4145, ext. 5000, or e-
mail special.markets@perseusbooks.com.

ISBN 978-0-7624-4452-6

Library of Congress Control Number: 2012930968

E-book ISBN 978-0-7624-4502-8

9   8   7   6   5   4   3   2   1
Digit on the right indicates the number of this printing

Cover design by Joshua McDonnell
Interior design by Joshua McDonnell
Edited by Geoff Stone

Typography: Akzidens, Avenir, and Bembo

Running Press Book Publishers
2300 Chestnut Street
Philadelphia, PA 19103-4371

Visit us on the Web!
www.runningpress.com

To my wife Sue and my three children, Matthew, Emma, and Grace, without whose patience, support, and most of all love, the completion of this book would not have been possible. Also, for my dad Jim who instilled in me my lifelong love of the game of baseball.

—KEVIN NEARY

For my dad, who not only taught me about the game of baseball but gave me my passion for it. To my children Katie and Sean, to whom I hope to pass on the same love of baseball. And to my husband Eric, for his patience through it all!

—LEIGH A. TOBIN

There might be 55,000 fans in the stand but you can always hear your dad's voice.

—JEFF FRANCOEUR,
OUTFIELDER FOR THE KANSAS CITY ROYALS

CONTENTS

CONTENTS

CONTENTS

◇ ACKNOWLEDGMENTS ◇

Robert Astle, Steve Barr (Little League International), Frank Blum (WALT DISNEY WORLD Company), Brian Britten (Detroit Tigers), Peter Chase (Chicago Cubs), Brandon Cohen, Chris Costello, Chad Crunk (University of Arkansas), Joe Cuomo (New York Mets), Joe Dier (Mississippi State University), Brenda Earhart, Johnny Ferrero, Terry Francona, Pam Ganley (Boston Red Sox), Coddy Granum, Brad Hainje (Atlanta Braves), Dave Haller (Tampa Bay Rays), Andrew Heydt (Tampa Bay Rays), Dani Holmes-Kirk (Chicago Cubs), Brad Horn (National Baseball Hall of Fame & Museum), John Horne (National Baseball Hall of Fame & Museum), Jay Horowitz (New York Mets), Mike Huff (Georgia Tech), Josh Ishoo (San Diego Padres), Greg Jones, James Earl Jones, Dave Kaczmarczyk, Doug Kemp (Philadelphia Phillies), Amanda Koch (Philadelphia Phillies), Scott Littlefield (WALT DISNEY WORLD Company), Kendall Loyd, Michelle Marks (Pete Mayta, Cheryl Meeks, Adrienne Midgley (Atlanta Braves), Warren Miller (San Diego Padres), Hal Morningstar, James Neary, Veronica Neary, Dr. Gary Nelson, Tom O'Reilly (WALT DISNEY WORLD Company), Candy Owens, Veronica Owens, Paul Perrello, Bret Picciolo (San Diego Padres), Matthew Ratner (Florida International University), Carmen Rios-Molina, Matt Rivlin (Tampa Bay Rays), Phil Alden Robinson, Tom Rodowsky (Walt Disney), Linda Rolen, Carol and Ed Rogers, Dave Schofield, Geoffrey Stone, Bob Thomas (Florida State University), Rick Thompson (Detroit Tigers), John Timberlake (Philadelphia Phillies), Jim Trdinich (Pittsburgh Pirates), Mike Tuohey (WALT DISNEY WORLD Company), Rick Vaughn (Tampa Bay Rays), Tom Whiteway (Tampa Bay Rays), Casey Wilcox (Arizona Diamondbacks), Shana Wilson (San Diego Padres), Judy Wolf, Melody Yount (St. Louis Cardinals), and Ed Zausch.

IN MEMORY OF GARY CARTER WHO
REPRESENTED "THE KID" IN ALL OF US

◇ FOREWORD ◇

I have been involved in baseball my entire life. My father was a major league player, I was a major league player, and now I manage in the major leagues.

My father, John "Tito" Francona, was an outfielder/first baseman in the majors (as was I) from 1956 to 1970. My career started out strong (in 1981), but I'd like to think my knees prevented me from having a more successful playing career. I was done playing in 1990 and moved into the coaching and managing ranks in 1991. The White Sox organization gave me opportunities to manage in the minors, but in 1996 I got my big break. General Manager Lee Thomas hired me to be the manager for the Philadelphia Phillies; it was my first big league managing job.

I met a lot of great people in Philadelphia, many of whom I am still friends with to this day. The team didn't have the best results, but I learned a lot and gained experience. Many of the people I met there helped me get through the daily requests, avoid pitfalls, and provided the basis for my future success. One of those people was Leigh A. Tobin, the little spitfire PR person who was by my side through my four years there.

"Leigh-Leigh" never got flustered. She treated everyone in that clubhouse with respect, which is why I think they respected her in return. She advised me on interviews, anticipated my statistical needs, would listen to my rants without judgment, was firm, but remained a rock through it all.

I was hired as the Boston Red Sox manager in 2004, probably the biggest move and most thrilling year of my career. It was the first of two World Championships I experienced there. And it was shortly after that year that Leigh-Leigh introduced me to Kevin Neary.

Kevin is a fascinating person who can tell a story better than anyone I have ever met. He told me about his idea for this book and got me thinking about my father. Looking back, when I was growing up I think I probably took my dad for granted. It wasn't until I moved out on my own that I realized how lucky I was.

One of my first memories was traveling with my dad a little bit when he was playing during those summer months. My dad was special . . . he was a major league player, but he was always a dad first to me. He was gone a lot with his job, but somehow he managed to make me feel important. He encouraged me to try my best and to enjoy the game. He never put a lot of pressure on me—he cared more about *me*—and to this day I am proud of him . . . and I hope I learned a lot about being a dad, so I can pass it on to my kids.

That is what makes this a special book. Every kid has special memories about his father—funny stories, vivid memories, great advice—and this is a great way for many major leaguers to share those stories and honor the men who helped us get here. (By the way, the best advice I received from my dad was to respect the game, respect the people in the game, and enjoy the competitiveness of the game.)

When my son Nick was in Little League, I was right there for him, as my dad was for me and, hopefully, Nick will be for his son one day. For us, baseball is just the means to a stronger father/son bond that is passed from generation to generation.

—TERRY FRANCONA

I need to begin with an admission . . . I am a baseball fan and I have my father to thank for that.

They say that history begins the year you were born but when you have a father that loves the game of baseball, history has no defined boundary. My dad would always remind me of the great players he grew up watching, Bob Feller, Warren Spahn, Joe DiMaggio, Stan Musial, Roy Campanella, Willie Mays, and of course Ted Williams. He would also talk about the great players who played the game before them, Ty Cobb, Walter Johnson, Grover Alexander, Rogers Hornsby, Lou Gehrig, Lefty Grove, and of course "The Babe."

To the casual observer the game of baseball is played by two teams, on a field, preferably grass, with batters and fielders all competing in an effort to outscore their opponent in a given nine innings of play. Three strikes make an out, first base is ninety feet away, and the pitcher's mound is sixty feet, six inches from home. Sounds simple, doesn't it? Yet the game we call baseball for many is much more complicated, involving strategy and a sound game plan. And for some, the game takes on a somewhat philosophical approach. To these special individuals, "Baseball Is Life," so says the popular expression.

Baseball is truly a game of tradition, heritage, and that of honoring excellence. And, I guess when my own son, Matthew, and my daughters, Emma and Grace, who I do coach in baseball, get a little older it will be my job and responsibility, as my dad did, to educate them on those same traditions regarding baseball and the greats who have played the game.

When I was a kid, I played baseball every chance I got. I loved spring and summer because that meant it was baseball season. Growing up we played baseball around the neighborhood, as well as a variety of games all inspired by baseball. I remember we used to play a game called half-ball. It involved a broomstick as a bat and a ball appropriately called a pimple ball we would then cut in two equal halves and use to compete on the street or in a back alley.

So many people have asked me over the years as I was collecting my research and writing this book, "Is this a book about baseball?" The answer is "Yes." But, it's less a book about baseball and more a book about the relationships between fathers and their sons.

The common thread that connects each of these stories is that it involves a major league ballplayer who had a father who served in a coaching capacity during his life. The book itself is designed to highlight the positive relationships of these fathers and their sons who have played, or currently play, the game of baseball. Each story describes the influence their father had on their baseball careers, their approach to life, and/or their own relationship with their families.

As you read each player's story you will discover that every situation between father and player is unique as you might expect. Yet, there are subtle nuances that seem to connect each of the stories. What you will quickly discover is that behind every great ballplayer is an equally great father, who loves his son and shares with him the love of the game. A father, who was able to connect with his son, made the sacrifices when he needed to, and shared with him a common dream. I am sorry to say, however, that this book is not a blueprint on how to become a major league ballplayer.

This leads me to the next question, "Where did I gain the inspiration for the book?" For inspiration, I turned to two sources. As I watched the Little League World Series in 2005 I got my first source of inspiration. I began to wonder if the best players are oftentimes the coach's son. This seemed to be the case with the Maitland, Florida, Little League team, which featured Dante Bichette Jr. and Tanner Stanley. Both, in this case, the sons of former major league ball players. After a few calls to the Little League World Series in Williamsport, Pennsylvania, and to the National Baseball Hall of Fame and Museum in Cooperstown, New York, my suspicions were confirmed. Each organization provided many examples of players who they knew were at one point coached by their father.

One such player was catching great Gary Carter. When he was inducted into the Baseball Hall of Fame, he began by telling the thousands in attendance that, "My parents can't be here today in person, but I know that they are smiling down from heaven today, because they have the best seats in the house." He continued and gave a glowing account of his own father Jim, "He was always there for me. He coached me in Little League, Pony League, and American Legion and also supported me in any other sport I played, constantly encouraging me. His favorite time of year was spring training, when he'd come and visit the family and watch a few games. He would go early with me to the ballpark and would stay until the end. He just couldn't get enough baseball."

So, there I was poised and ready to write this book. And for someone like me who is firmly planted in the concept of tradition, it seemed only fitting that my first interview for the book would be with Gary Carter, the player who quickly came to be, in my mind, the quintessential example of a son who was coached by his father. For over sixteen years Gary Carter's father was his coach. "My father always reminded me to keep a level head, to keep focused, stay on track, and understand that I was given many God given gifts," said a reflective Carter. "My father was always a part of my life and he was a great role model for me. I was his son, and my dad was my idol and my best friend." admitted Carter. "My greatest honor after my nineteen-year professional career was to be honored by the National Baseball Hall of Fame. I know during my Induction Ceremony speech my father was looking over my right shoulder and my mom was looking over my left shoulder."

Very quickly what I discovered was that the book was developing its own personality. I remember very early on in the writing project a media relations official by the name of Chris Costello from the Tampa Bay Rays approached me during an interview session and said, "Please let our home (Tampa) be your home for your American League interviews." Shortly after that exchange, the Atlanta Braves and the Philadelphia Phillies made similar acknowledgments. I never knew who I was going to interview when I stepped into any clubhouse. There is certainly no media guide or documentation that says, "Played Little League and Pony League from ages six years old and up and was coached by his dad." Every time I entered a clubhouse I knew I had to ask the question to every player I came into contact with.

I got several "no's" but not of the nasty sort. In most cases the player would say, "No, my dad couldn't coach me because he was working all of the time." And then they usually followed it up with an "It's not like he didn't want to be my coach!" Many players that I came into contact with, Tim Hudson, Chase Utley, Randy Johnson, Ivan Rodriguez, A. J. Pierzynski, Gary Sheffield, Paul Konerko, David Ortiz, and Ryan Howard, to name just a few, fell into this category. That hopefully answers yet another question I would often get about the book, "Why didn't you interview this player or that player?" Certainly, I would have loved to interview the players mentioned, and so many more, but they didn't fit the paradigm of being coached by their father.

One of the most interesting responses from a player that I came into contact with was pitcher John Smoltz. I asked John the same question I asked all the players, "Was your dad ever your coach growing up?" Smoltz replied, "No, my father was a musician, and he wanted me to be a musician, too." I replied back, "I guess that is why you are such a virtuoso on the mound." I think he appreciated the compliment.

Another interesting situation occurred with baseball great Alex Rodriguez. I remember when I interviewed Derek Jeter. Like so many players, Derek was very excited about the opportunity to talk about his father. In fact, I had to interview Derek twice because each time we ran out of time with the interview session. One of the days I interviewed Derek, Alex Rodriguez was sitting across from us and suiting up. Alex seemed very interested and fascinated at Derek's recounts and stories about his father. I remember, when I finished with Derek, out of curiosity I turned to Alex and said, "Mr. Rodriguez may I ask you the same question? Were you ever coached by your father?" He admitted that his father did not coach him. I apologized to him, stating the parameters of the book and my inability to interview him. I wished him continued success and the very best. Alex then stood up, extended his hand, and said, "No, thank you and God bless!" I think Alex truly enjoyed listening to Derek's own account of his father and the impact he had on his life.

Over the years, I've had players laugh with me and cry with me as they relate the stories of growing up being the coach's son. In fact, I remember one player said to me, "I haven't talked to my dad in over twenty years, but I owe him everything and am hoping your book brings us back together."

A question that has often come up during the writing of this book is, "Were most of the fathers featured in this book perceived as hard on their sons and pushed them into the sport?" The answer consistently of those that I have interviewed has been, "No." Only one player admitted, "My dad was the Little League coach from hell but looking back at my career I owe him everything."

The quickest interview I ever did was with pitcher Mike Hampton. I asked Hampton if he, too, was coached by his father growing up. Hampton was off to the trainer's room but quickly responded, "Yes!" I then asked, "At what age did he start his coaching of you as a player?" "At the age of four," replied the hurried Hampton. And finally, "When did he stop coaching you?" Laughing at my question, Hampton said, "He is still my coach!"

When I talked to some old-time ballplayers, like Al Kaline and Ferguson Jenkins, I remember asking them the same question, "Did your father ever coach you in Little League?" The answer I received was basically the same, "No, he didn't. He was working all of the time and the most he would do was to drop me off at the recreation center so I could play ball."

The second source for my inspiration is my own father, Jim. Even though my father was never my coach growing up, he taught me to love the game and most important to respect it, a common lesson he also taught each of his children about life.

My father taught us to treat others how you would like to be treated yourself. And, that it's perfectly acceptable to say "Thank you" and "You're welcome" whenever the occasion arises.

Growing up in a city like Philadelphia was pretty similar to growing up in other big cities or even any small town. You loved your own hometown team or the team you followed and subsequently despised all the rest.

However, if the American League team had a cool uniform, then that was usually a good enough reason to like them. Growing up in the 1970s, the Oakland Athletics immediately come to mind. The A's wore solid green or solid gold jerseys, with contrasting white pants, at a time when most of the other teams wore all white uniforms at home and a gray uniform when the team was on the road. Plus they had some pretty awe-some teams back then that included players like Bert Campaneris, Rollie Fingers, Catfish Hunter, and Reggie Jackson.

And, I don't think there was a kid out there during the 1970s that didn't want to pitch like Vida Blue, given his exaggerated delivery on the mound.

And speaking of the Athletics, many of you may or may not know Oakland was not their original home. Prior to Oakland they played in Kansas City and Philadelphia. I remember my father telling me how he cried the day the Athletics left town. "Why couldn't it have been the Phillies," he would say. The reason: the Athletics consistently fielded a good team over the years while the Phillies generally spent more time in the proverbial cellar.

I remember my uncle and father would often debate which Philadelphia Athletics player was the best or which player had the greatest impact on the game. Despite their disagreements, they would always agree on one thing, Cornelius McGillicuddy Sr., better known as Connie Mack. "Now, there was a manager!" they would say. And to his credit, Connie Mack was a manage-rial icon and still remains so today. Anyone who has been able to capture and win nine American League pennants, five World Series Championships titles, and post over 3,700 Major League victories has to be doing something right.

As time went by, my father accepted the Athletics departure and welcomed the Phillies as his team. My father was alternately simple and yet complex. Like the famous Will Rogers, he never met a man he didn't like. Except when it came to Philadelphia Phillies managers, he never met one he liked. Perhaps this was his way of never blaming the player for the team's poor perform-ances. The manager was always at fault. And maybe it was his own upbringing of never blaming the common man. He particu-larly loved those players he considered "blue collar." My father was a huge fan of Ted Williams, Ernie Banks, and Al Kaline.

For thirty-nine years my father got up early and went to work driving a trolley in the city of Philadelphia. I guess this is why he got along with people so well, considering the number of passengers he encountered on a daily basis.

My father taught his children to love their family, to cherish their time together, to laugh, and most important to enjoy life. My father also taught us the simple things in life, like doing a day's work for a day's pay and the importance of remembering where you come from. I remember spending quite a bit of time with my father at the depot when I was younger. I guess you can say my father was participating in the "Bring your child to work day" even before it became fashionable. And, what kid wouldn't have enjoyed riding the trolley with their dad at the wheel and then going back to the depot to meet his buddies.

My father loved his God, his family, and his country. He was a part of the great working class that helped build this country.

My father was, by all accounts, part of the greatest generation that has graced this country. He fought in World War II in both the European and Asian campaigns and watched his friends die heroes and rejoiced after victory. Yet, my father was a first generation immigrant. Both of his parents were born in a small town in County Mayo, Ireland.

I learned to work hard and push myself to be the best from my father. And as I get older, I am proud to say that I find myself turning into my father. There is so much of him that is now a part of me.

As I think back on the lifetime of lessons that I learned from my parents, I can only smile and say "Thank you." Just like Hall of Famer Gary Carter reflected upon in his own induction speech, I know my parents are smiling down from heaven today.

My only hope is that you enjoy the following stories as much as I did researching and putting them together. My other wish is that someday the Phillies play the Athletics in the World Series. I know my dad and mom will have the best seats in the house. I can honestly say who he'd root for in the series is anyone's guess . . . heaven only knows.

◆ MOISES ALOU ◆

Moises Alou has baseball in his blood—literally.

The Alou family has a rich baseball history. The Dominican brothers—Felipe, Jesus, and Matty Alou—all played Major League Baseball. Moise's father, Felipe, was arguably the best of the brothers. A three-time All-Star and two-time National League leader in hits, Felipe also served as manager for the Montreal Expos (1992–2001) and San Francisco Giants (2003–06) after his playing career was over.

"My life has always been around the game," said Moises. "I remember going with my dad all the time to the ballpark. I remember spending a lot of time in a big-league clubhouse. Baseball has always been a part of my life. It was always wonderful spending time with my father."

Despite coming from a storied baseball family, Moises did not play organized baseball until he went to college at Canada College in Redwood City, California. He had impressive skills, however, and became the second overall selection in the June 1986 draft when the Pittsburgh Pirates chose him.

An outfielder, just like his father and uncles before him, Moises became a six-time All-Star and a 1997 World Series champion (with the Florida Marlins). He was lucky enough to have his father manage him twice in the majors—first with the Expos (1992–96), and then with the Giants (2005–06).

"I remember I was fourteen years old," said Moises, thinking back to one of his favorite baseball memories. "It was in Montreal and my dad was a coach. I was in the clubhouse getting autographs. I even got one from my favorite player, Gary Carter. But what made this a good memory for me was that twelve years later, Gary Carter was a teammate of mine! Baseball has always been a great experience for me."

It is possible that there will be another generation of Alous playing Major League Baseball. "I have three boys," said Moises, of his sons Percio, Kirby, and Moises Jr., "and they love being around the clubhouse, too. And, hopefully, one day, they can tell their own stories about their father."

◆ GARRETT ATKINS ◆

California native Garrett Atkins said he was a typical coach's son growing up. "My dad was my coach pretty much all the way up to high school. He began in player pitch and he has always been there in some capacity to help out," Atkins began.

"I remember the hours he worked with me over the years, just with hitting balls to me on the weekend. My dad always told me that he wanted me to play the game right. So being the son of the coach, he always tried to get me to set a good example, to work harder than anyone else, and most important to play the game right."

The first and third baseman attended UCLA after graduating from University High School in 1997. At UCLA, he played and roomed with Chase Utley (the 2011 second baseman for the Philadelphia Phillies) and became the school's only three-time All-American (1998–2000).

Atkins was selected by the Colorado Rockies in the 5th round of the June 2000 draft. He made his major-league debut on August 3, 2003, and has gone on to play over seven seasons with the Rockies and Baltimore Orioles.

Atkins said his dad was always there for him, through every level. "I don't always turn to my dad for advice anymore," admitted Atkins, "but it is nice to know he is always willing to give it. If I don't get a hit for a few games, he is on the phone calling me to give some advice. My dad can look at a box score tomorrow and know what I am doing wrong. If I'm not getting the hits I should, he always knows exactly what I am doing wrong. My dad always knew I had the talent and was always there to keep me going and working hard."

◆ ROCCO BALDELLI ◆

Rocco Baldelli loves baseball and loves to talk about his father—a perfect combination for this book.

"My dad coached me from T-ball all the way up until I was thirteen years old," said Baldelli. "He officially stopped being my coach when I went on to high school, but he is still unofficially my coach to this day.

"He gives me advice even before I ask for it," the six foot four outfielder continued. "I started playing in high school, and he always had advice to share then and even today . . . and I still listen."

Baldelli shared the advice his dad continues to share with him. "He always tells me the same thing, even to this day. I'll go home in the off-season and he always tells me to move closer to the plate, swing harder, and keep your head in. It sounds like Little League still, but he's been saying the same thing since I was five years old. He always has to remind me that I keep pulling my head out.

"My dad also taught me to work hard because, as he would say, 'You're only going to get one shot at it. You don't want it to be over and think to yourself, did you give it your all?'"

Baldelli's father clearly means the world to him. The Rhode Island native recalled some stories of growing up with his father. "I have a picture of me with a big, red Wiffle bat in my hands. I used to play with it in the backyard and my dad always used to pitch to me. Even when we moved to a house with a big backyard, we would play every day in the summer.

"When I was in high school," Baldelli continued, "he even set up a batting cage in the basement of his store. It was in this old building with thick walls and big old beams. It was the perfect width for a batting cage. It all started when the batting cage we had in our backyard collapsed because of the weight of the snow. So we took the netting off and put it downstairs and nailed it to the walls. We put up a makeshift mound and a makeshift home plate. My dad even threw some fake turf on the floor, installed some spotlights . . . it was just perfect. It's still there when I go home in the off-season and I get to hit there each time."

After a successful athletic and academic career at Bishop Hendricken High School, Baldelli was selected by the Tampa

Bay Devil Rays in the first round (6th overall) of the June 2000 draft. Three years later, he was in the big leagues as the starting center fielder for the Devil Rays.

"It was Opening Day in 2003," recalled Baldelli. "It was here in Tampa and it was my very first game and my dad was there. It was against the Red Sox, and being from Rhode Island and just forty-five minutes away from Boston, he was still rooting just for me. He always roots for me."

The proud father follows his son as closely as he can. "He gets that special television package and watches all the games," said Baldelli with a grin. "My family gets together with everyone and they all watch. He is a devoted fan of just me. My dad has always been there for me and he is proud of all his kids. Just listening to my dad talk is enough for me."

◆ CLINT BARMES ◆

"I have been coached by my dad ever since I picked up a bat, even before Little League, and up to the point I reached college," said Clint Barmes a major-league infielder from Indiana. "My first year in Little League I was seven years old in a machine-pitch league and that's when it all started in organized play. Over the years my dad practiced and worked with me a lot."

Barmes credits his father with teaching him the value of hard work. "He taught me about the work ethic. He taught me how to play the game. My dad would always be on me about playing the game hard, to go out and have fun, and to give it my all. Over the years, baseball was all that I knew," he stated. "If I didn't go on to be a ballplayer, then I would have been a carpenter."

For Barmes, family always came first. "I would say my family members were my idols and have always been a big part of my life," he said. "My dad was more into playing with us instead of sitting and watching a game. I grew up as a Cardinals fan, and I got to go to one or two games when I was little. My baseball hero at that time was Ozzie Smith. . . . I still love watching him."

Barmes graduated from Lincoln High School in 1997. "When I was in high school I got a couple of offers from a few junior colleges," said Barmes, who went to Olney Central Community College in Illinois for two years on a scholarship, before heading to Indiana State University. "After my freshman year in college, I got a few more looks and I started thinking that becoming a big-league player may happen. By my third year in college I got even more playing time and even stronger in the game and my dream started to become even more of a reality."

Barmes took the next step when the Colorado Rockies selected him in the 10th round of the June 2000 draft. "Once I got into professional ball, I learned a lot about the game from some of the older players who were on the team," Barmes recalled. "I'd bring what I learned back to my dad and we again learned together. It was things he might not have thought of. But for the most part, my dad taught me the basics and he was the one who got me involved in the game. My dad helped convince me to work hard and to put in the time to get here. It was my dad who I first discussed being a pro player with."

Barmes recalled a story that symbolized his family's loyalty and commitment to him. "My family has always been a big part of my life," he insisted. "The best story I remember was when I began my professional career. My grandparents drove out from Indiana to Portland, Oregon, to see me play in the minor leagues. My grandmother didn't want to fly. They took three days to get there. The next day I got called up, so they missed me playing in Portland. I called them from the airport and I said to them, 'I've got good news and bad news. The bad news is that I won't be in Portland tonight. The good news is I got called up to the next level and will be in Asheville, North Carolina.' So my grandparents turned the car around that same day. Three days later, they met me in Asheville. They have always made the time to see me play."

The six foot one infielder achieved his dream on September 5, 2003, when he made his major-league debut with a start at shortstop for Colorado against the Los Angeles Dodgers. He spent almost eight years in the majors with the Rockies before joining his current team, the Houston Astros.

"I feel like I have a great relationship with my dad," Barmes concluded in an interview before his father died. "I have always enjoyed talking baseball with my dad. We talk about every aspect of the game and over the years we've both been able to learn together."

(Barmes's father, Barry, passed away from lung cancer in October 2010.)

◆ DAVID BELL ◆

When you are a member of a rare group—a three-generation Major League Baseball family—the odds are long that your father would be able to be your coach growing up. However, bet against the odds with the Bell family.

Meet the Bells: grandfather Gus, a fifteen-year MLB outfielder who played mainly with the Cincinnati Reds and Pittsburgh Pirates and was a four-time All-Star; father Buddy, an eighteen-year major leaguer who played mainly for the Cleveland Indians, Texas Rangers, and Cincinnati Reds, was a five-time All-Star, and earned six Gold Gloves for his excellent play at third base, then was also a coach in the major leagues as well as a manager for nine seasons; and son David, a twelve-year major leaguer who played mainly for the St. Louis Cardinals, Seattle Mariners, and Philadelphia Phillies, and was known for his professionalism, steady bat, and reliable play at third base.

"Growing up, my father was never able to coach me in baseball," the youngest Bell clarified. "But he coached me in basketball. My dad coached me and my brothers." (David's brothers, Mike and Ricky, were also drafted by major-league teams, but only Mike made it to the majors for one season with the Cincinnati Reds in 2002.) "He was eventually my baseball coach when I played in Cleveland for the Indians."

"My dad taught us a lot, not only about basketball, but how to compete and what it meant to be a part of a team—all the good things that carry over to baseball," the usually soft-spoken Bell said.

Growing up around major-league clubhouses gave Bell a chance to see baseball players from another side. "There were always players who were really my favorites," he said, then added with a smile, "but my dad overshadowed anyone else. I watched him from the moment I woke up to the time I went to bed . . . and I tried to be just like him."

The greatest advice Bell received from his idol and father: "Have fun, hustle, and do your best. They are the things that seem pretty simple, but are very important."

He is still close to his father to this day. "I talk to him once or twice a week during the season and in the off-season we spend a lot of time together."

What about the other generation, his grandfather? "I never saw him play," said Bell, "but I spent a lot of quality time with him and we were very close. He was able to be around for my baseball games when my dad wasn't able to. He was also a big influence in my life."

The closeness of the family is illustrated by the final story David shared about his father when he was growing up. "I remember my dad was playing in Texas and I was in Little League," Bell began. "Players get to the ballpark around two or three o'clock. They take batting practice between four and five o'clock when the game is at seven.

"Well, between five and seven there is a little down time. Once batting practice was over my dad would run to his car, while still in uniform, and drive to my field and watch the game. And no one knew he was there.

"It was really nice," he continued. "I knew he was there and it was a great feeling I think for him to be there. And just so we would know that he was there, when we did something good, he would honk the horn. We then knew he was there watching us."

This tradition actually began with Bell's grandfather. Gus would make the same effort to get to Buddy's games and honked the horn in the same fashion to let him know that he was there and approved of his play. So will David do the same for his son? "Yeah, I probably will," he grinned.

◆ LANCE BERKMAN ◆

"If you want to be good, you've got to pay the price."

That piece of advice was the greatest lesson All-Star Lance Berkman learned from his father. The phrase became a mantra during his youth—and beyond. "It has been a foundation of mine that has stuck with me all my life," Berkman said. "Whether I'm hitting from the cage or off the golf tee, you need to do the things you need to do to be successful."

Berkman's father was his coach from age seven to almost twelve. "However," noted the big first baseman, "my dad was always a coach of mine, even though he did not have that official title. He was always the guy I learned stuff off of."

He continues to learn from his father to this day. "My father has been instrumental in my career and even now I call him for advice. I talk to him about the game and stuff like that. The good thing about my dad is that he is smart enough to realize I am at a level of play now that he isn't able to compare to . . . and that I probably learn through experience more about the mechanics of the swing, and what you can and can't do, than what he can offer from an advice standpoint."

"But," Berkman continued, "the mental side of the game is a different story. My dad is a very good mental coach. He is always somebody I'll call and talk to, especially when I'm not doing well. He is always that guy who can really help pump you up and has been great for me in that capacity."

Berkman was—and is—passionate about the game of baseball, something his father recognized in him at a young age. He explained with a story: "My dad really invested a lot of time in me. We had this batting cage out in the country. We'd go out there about every weekend—Saturdays and Sundays—and just hit. That's where I honed my swing. I remember I'd get mad at him at times when I didn't want to be out there, but he'd drag me out there to do this or that. You know when you are a kid it wasn't always the first thing on your mind. But looking back, I am so glad he made that effort." That effort paid off in big ways for Berkman, who has been a professional baseball player since the Houston Astros drafted him in 1997. A major leaguer since 1999, he played almost twelve seasons (nearly his entire career) with the Astros, which was great for his parents who live about two and a half hours away from Houston.

"My father was there for my first game," Berkman recalled fondly, of the July 16, 1999, meeting with Detroit. "He has gone to a lot of games and he is always there for Opening Day. I know he takes a lot of pride and pleasure in watching the games.

"He also feels like he has to motivate me, even to this day," Berkman added with a smile. "Then again, that's what dads are for!"

♦ WILSON BETEMIT ♦

Wilson Betemit grew up in the Dominican Republic, where baseball rules the day. That is why his love of basketball was not as encouraged as it may have been in the United States.

"My father was always my coach," began Betemit. "He taught me everything I know about the game of baseball.

"Most of all," he continued, "my father taught me the concept of hard work. I remember when I was a kid I didn't like baseball as much as I liked basketball. Whenever he saw me begin to play basketball, he'd say, 'It's time for baseball!' And then it was time to play baseball.

"I always knew the best way to get my father's attention was to start playing basketball," he added with a big grin.

Betemit signed with the Atlanta Braves when he was just fourteen years old. He made his major-league debut on September 18, 2001, at the age of nineteen. The infielder has played with the Atlanta Braves, Los Angeles Dodgers, New York Yankees, Chicago White Sox, Detroit Tigers, and Kansas City Royals in his career.

Despite Wilson Betemit being forced to move around a lot due to his career, his father still stays in touch with his major-league son. With a big smile on his face, Betemit said, "I still talk to my father almost every day! He comes to see me play as much as he can."

Fortunately, the six foot three switch-hitter said he has gotten over his brief love affair with basketball. "I'm good now," Betemit said. "I've played baseball since I was five years old, but it wasn't until I was thirteen that I played baseball all the time. I thank my father for all that he did to help me to love this game."

◆ JEREMY BONDERMAN ◆

"My dad coached me pretty much all the time," said Jeremy Bonderman, a young man who made a very quick ascent to the major leagues.

"Probably one of my first baseball memories was of Little League and T-ball. My dad was my coach. We had all of my buddies on the same team and we had a lot of fun!" he recalled.

Bonderman is a rarity in that he was drafted in his junior year of high school—in June 2001 by the Oakland Athletics. He was traded to the Detroit Tigers the following season and made his Major League Baseball debut in a start against the Minnesota Twins at the ripe old age of twenty, on April 2, 2003.

"My dad attended my first start in the big leagues back in '03. He flew up with all my brothers. It was a fun time. I didn't pitch very well," Bonderman conceded, "but it was fun."

Going through so much in such a short period of time can be a challenge, which is why having a father to turn to for advice is comforting. "If I find myself struggling during the season, my dad is the guy I call. He is the one who can help me. Our father-and-son relationship is very strong," shared Bonderman.

"I talk to him quite a bit—at least two to three times a week. He is my mentor and the reason why I am here."

After a lot of early success, Bonderman faced some challenges due to injuries in 2008 and 2009. But he still managed to overcome them, thanks to the lessons he learned from his father, lessons he graciously shared. "Your father teaches you more about life than anything. He always told me, if you want to be someone special, then you gotta work hard and never give up and know there are going to be a lot of obstacles in your life. The strong survive. He always pushed me to be the best I can be."

◆ AARON BOONE ◆

When your father is a Major League Baseball player, odds are he will not be coaching your Little League team. Aaron Boone, grandson of former major leaguer Ray Boone, son of former major-league catcher Bob Boone, and younger brother to major leaguer Bret Boone, can attest to that. However, Aaron was coached by his dad in the major leagues when Bob managed him in Cincinnati for two and a half years.

Despite his father not officially coaching him at a young age, the young Boone learned volumes from him. "My brother and I were always around the game," Boone recalled. "We were very lucky. From a very early age our dad would take us to the ballpark all the time. Looking back at it now, it was an awesome way to grow up. My dad was always involved in our lives. We were lucky to do all that we did.

"I admired my parents the most growing up," he continued. "From a very early age I loved being around the park, being with my dad, and being around the guys. We always had our favorite players, and me and my brother loved baseball from the get-go."

His father, Bob, is still involved in baseball, as assistant general manager and vice president of player development for the Washington Nationals. Aaron still calls his dad and seeks his advice all the time, but the greatest advice he received from his father was something the elder Boone reiterated to him numerous times. "My dad would always say, 'Do something you love and do it to the best of your ability,'" said Boone. "I take that wherever I go."

After a twelve-year Major League Baseball career, Boone retired. But in thinking back to June 1997, when he made his major-league debut, he recalled his father's reaction. "I remember my dad telling me, when I told him I was going to get called up, to 'Spit in their eye!'" Boone recalled fondly. "It was an expression he used since I was little, which means: don't be afraid and show them what you've got!"

◆ JOE BORCHARD ◆

Outfielder Joe Borchard was a first round selection (12th overall) of the Chicago White Sox out of Stanford University in 2000. But he was not the first member of his family to become a professional baseball player. His father Joe was selected by the Kansas City Royals in the 1969 draft.

Joe Borchard credited his father with sharing his baseball knowledge with him. "My dad began coaching me when I was a young kid and all the way up through Little League," said Borchard. "He did a great job. My dad helped me to become the ballplayer that I am and made many sacrifices along the way.

"My father taught me all about baseball," he continued, "and most of all how to be a good dad . . . now that I'm a father these days. He taught me how important it is to support and to raise a family. It is nice to have a father like him to look back on. It is important to think about what it meant then and what it means now. Back when I was a little kid, it was just him simply throwing balls to me and him trying to help me become a better ballplayer.

"When you think about it now, you think of the time he spent and the tremendous effort he put into it. I am so fortunate for the time he spent with me. If you look at it that way, it allows you to have a whole new perspective on life and how great a dad he was!"

The outgoing Californian reminisced about his earliest memories of baseball with his father. "I remember him playing Wiffle ball with me and having catches all of the time," recalled Borchard. "It was a lot of fun. Just to remember how much he enjoyed it really was a neat thing for me."

Borchard, who is married and has a young daughter, said his father's teachings went beyond the baseball diamond. "The greatest lesson my dad taught me goes back to the whole issue of family again," he said. "He was very good at showing me how critical it was to spend time with your family and how important it is to support them. It was always important for him to spend the time he did with his kids and that was the greatest lesson he has left with me."

Borchard said his father "put his money where his mouth is"

by showing his support of his son through his entire pro career. "My parents were there for my first major-league game," recalled Borchard of his September 2, 2002, debut. "It was in Chicago when I first got called up and they were there. But they were always there.

"Prior to getting the call-up in the big leagues, they had been with me when I was in Triple-A. My first game was on Labor Day, and it was pretty exciting for me and for them. It was a pretty cool time for me and it was great having them share in that."

◆ JEFF BRANTLEY ◆

Jeff Brantley is one of the most engaging people in the game of baseball.

The retired fourteen-year MLB reliever and current broadcaster for the Cincinnati Reds always has a good story for anyone who listens. So needless to say, he had a great story about his father, who coached him throughout his childhood in the South.

"My dad was my coach and catcher all of my life," Brantley began. "Every day we'd go out and have a catch." Every session began the same way—with Jeff's father saying, "Show me what you got!"

This routine went on for years and Jeff's throwing ability got stronger and stronger. Despite Brantley's improved abilities and increased velocity, his father remained his coach and catcher.

Brantley attended Mississippi State University, where he was a member of the 1985 team that went to the College World Series, the same year he was selected in the 6th round of the June draft by the San Francisco Giants.

"I remember it was my first semester break and I got the opportunity to come home," Brantley recalled the first year of his college. "My dad asked me to have a catch. As always, we went out in the back. I went back to pitch and my dad crouched down to catch. Then my dad said the usual, 'Show me what you got!' So I wound up and threw my first pitch. It was a fastball," Brantley confessed. "The ball soared so fast by my dad's head that he never moved a muscle. My dad then took off his mitt, placed it on the ground in front of him, stood up, and walked into the house.

"I was eighteen years old and I thought to myself, 'Did I do something wrong?'" Brantley continued. "So I ran into the house to find my dad. I found him sitting on the sofa with his hands over his eyes crying. Again, I thought I did something wrong. So I said to him 'Dad did I do anything wrong?'"

"'You didn't do anything wrong,' he said. 'Then dad, what's the matter?' I asked. My dad then said, 'Today was the day I realized I can no longer have a catch with my son.'"

♦ REID BRIGNAC ♦

"I started to play T-ball when I was four years old," said Tampa Bay Rays shortstop Reid Brignac. "I was one of the youngest kids on the team. I batted left and I used to hit the ball well, and sometimes to the fence. Eventually, the other team would put a shift on me, moving everyone to the right side of the field. My dad would then yell out to me, 'Hey boy, turn around and hit right-handed.' I'd turn around and hit the ball to the other wall and run around the bases. It was kind of fun."

Brignac went to St. Amant High School in Louisiana, where he lettered in football and baseball, and earned academic honors with a 3.5 GPA. He was set to attend Louisiana State University on a scholarship when the Rays selected him in the 2nd round of the June 2004 draft. He decided to forego college and start his professional career.

The self-confident Cajun's father, Phillip, coached him in Dixie Baseball (the area's equivalent of Little League). "My dad was a big influence on me," said Brignac. "He taught me about work ethic—to work hard every chance you get. My dad would always say, 'If you want to be a good piano player, you've got to play the piano as much as you can. If you want to be a good teacher, you've got to go to school and read plenty of books and study. If you want to be a good baseball player, you've got to practice the game as much as you can.'"

Brignac worked hard on his baseball skills, particularly on his defense, throughout his minor-league career and improved at every level—enough to be brought up to the majors on July 4, 2008, for a game against the Kansas City Royals. He stuck in the majors in 2010 and became the regular shortstop for the Rays by 2011. "My parents both came for my first game in 2008 and they still come to a lot of games," he said. "They love it and enjoy it. My dad is almost retired, so when he does officially retire I know my parents will be here even more often."

Brignac said that even when his father is not there in person, he knows that his dad is only a phone call away. "I will definitely turn to my dad for advice the rest of my life," said Brignac. "The thing about it is that he has been on this Earth a whole lot longer than I have and he has been through a lot more situations, so he will always be someone I can always turn to. I am going through things now, in fact, that I've never faced before and he is just a quick phone call away. He is always there. My dad is that constant feel-good. He makes me feel good . . . just talking to him and getting his advice about something is all I ever need."

◆ JONATHAN BROXTON ◆

Major league closer Jonathan Broxton does his job succinctly and effectively, much like the way he speaks. His father was also succinct and effective in the advice he gave his son.

"My dad always taught me to be competitive and, most important, don't do anything stupid in life . . . especially when it meant doing something that could hurt your team," explained Broxton. "He would say, 'Remember your name is on the back of that jersey!'"

The Georgia native had his father as his coach from his T-ball years through middle school.

"Baseball has always been a part of my life," said Broxton. "I remember watching baseball with my dad all the time on the television. My dad played on this traveling softball team and I'd be with him as much as I could, watching him play. He was really good. I guess you can say that is why I've felt like I've been around the game so much."

Broxton was selected by the Los Angeles Dodgers in the 2nd round of the June 2002 draft out of Burke County High School, and it wasn't long before he was on his way to the major leagues.

He made his MLB debut on July 29, 2005, with the Dodgers against the St. Louis Cardinals. "My dad was there for my first game in Los Angeles back in 2005. It was something! I've always dreamed of getting to this level and it was great having him there to share it."

◆ MARK BUEHRLE ◆

The Chicago White Sox, and now the Miami Marlins, would have missed out on their left-handed All-Star if it hadn't been for the pitcher's father.

Mark Buehrle was cut from his high school baseball team in his freshman and sophomore years. "I wasn't even going to go out in my third year," confessed the lefty, "then my mom and dad sat down with me and encouraged me to go out in my third year. I remember my dad saying, 'We didn't raise a quitter!' and 'We want you to go out and give it one more shot.' And I did, and that is why I am here today."

Buehrle grew up in St. Charles, Missouri, where his father was never his head coach, "but he was on the bench as an assistant coach or in the stands, he was everywhere and he was always there to help me," he said.

Throughout his life Buehrle has had great aim and control, but despite that, he was not big enough to make the varsity baseball team at Francis Howell North High School. He began growing toward his ultimate six foot two height in his junior year, made the team, and by his senior year was the team's number two starter.

Buehrle was offered and accepted a baseball scholarship to Jefferson Junior College in Missouri. He went 8–0 in the spring of 1998, good enough that the Chicago White Sox took a chance selecting him in the 38th round of the June draft. They watched him have a good 8–4 season with a 2.70 ERA in 1999 and offered him a signing bonus, which he accepted in May of that year.

His career took off from that point, as he made his major-league debut in relief just over a year later on July 16, 2000. He made his first major-league start three days later in Minnesota. His parents missed his debut, but were there for his first start! "I had about thirty people there—mom, dad, brothers, sister, grandparents, everyone was there!" Buehrle recalled.

"I wasn't nervous that they were there, I was nervous because it was my first start pitching that day. When we went out to eat, a reporter misquoted or didn't understand me when I spoke about being with my family. He wrote that I was nervous eating with my family, when actually I said I was nervous about the game I was about to pitch."

Buehrle won his first start, moved into the starting rotation the following year, and has never looked back. He is a four-time All-Star, two-time Gold Glover, 2005 World Series Champion, and has thrown a no-hitter (April 18, 2007, vs. Texas) and a perfect game (July 23, 2009, vs. Tampa Bay). And still talks to his father after every game.

"My dad calls me after every start," he explained. "His words these days are more words of encouragement like, 'good start' or 'it looks like you had a lot of your good stuff today' or, when I know and he knows that I didn't have a good start, he would say 'you may not have had your good stuff today, but you're still there for a reason. Go get them next time and let this one pass.' So no matter whether I had a good or bad outing, he still always calls to share his 'never quit' philosophy."

The biggest conflict early on in the Missouri native's life was that he played for the White Sox, and his family was full of passionate St. Louis Cardinals fans. If the two teams met in the World Series, Buehrle is not sure who they would have rooted for. "Back in 2005, my family and I kind of joked about it when it came pretty close to that situation. I even asked some of my family the question, 'Hey who are you rooting for? . . . You better be rooting for me even though you are Cardinals fans!' They didn't answer, I can only hope that they would have rooted for me . . . I hope!" Buehrle said with a grin.

He joked, but he knows his family supports him. "My dad is my biggest cheerleader. All my family cheers me on. They wear White Sox gear to show their support—and being a Cardinals family that is a tough thing for them to do. Fortunately, they are in two different leagues and I think a lot of people down where my family is from want the White Sox to do better than the Cubs anyway."

◆ PAUL BYRD ◆

"The nicest guy in baseball," otherwise known as Paul Byrd, had a very supportive dad guiding him through his childhood years.

"My father was my coach in Little League and he helped me out a lot," said the Christian father of two. "But more so than just being my coach on the field in Little League, my dad worked with me. Practically every guy in this clubhouse has had a father or father figure who has spent the time and has had the interest in them at some point during their life. That is what my father did. More so than being my coach in Little League, my dad spent time with me and that was more important to me. He was always willing to have a catch with me, or throw batting practice, or even willing to catch me off the mound. He really enjoyed it. I don't think he was doing it for any other reason than because he loved me. I don't think he was doing it for some retirement policy or anything like that. Again, he did it because he loved me."

Parents will do many things for their children because they love them. Byrd's father didn't know much about baseball, but did his best to learn the game for the sake of his son. "My father allowed me to follow my heart," Byrd said. "I always loved and played baseball. My dad played basketball in college in Anderson, Indiana. He didn't know anything about baseball, but he knew it was in my heart and he allowed me to do what I wanted to do. He built that into me."

"My dad tried so hard," he continued with a smile. "I remember he even bought me this book, *Tom Seaver: The Art of Pitching* in order for me to improve. It was a pretty cool moment in my life."

Like many kids, when Byrd was growing up he had a favorite team and player. "I always pulled for Johnny Bench because I was in Louisville and Cincinnati wasn't that far away. So I grew up watching the Big Red Machine," Byrd recalled. "I remember going to a Reds game in 1977 and I got this George Foster bat, I was even one of the first 500 kids to get a black bat. I remember sleeping with that bat that night and thinking it was the greatest thing in the world. I know everyone's different, but I always loved baseball and I appreciate my dad for taking an interest in me."

Byrd's dad went above and beyond for his son, as the nearly twenty-year major leaguer recalled in one of his more vivid memories. "I remember after I signed with the Indians my dad was getting older and he still wanted to keep catching me," Byrd chuckled. "So one day he squatted down in the catcher's position and he put all the gear on. I was twenty-one years old and I know that he didn't want me to take it easy on him. I threw one pitch and it went right past his glove and hit him in the mask. The force of the throw turned his mask sideways on his head and this little piece of metal cut him across the top of his forehead. My dad stood up and said he was sorry he missed that one and proceeded to take off his mask as blood started pouring down his face.

"I'm twenty-one years old, and I thought I killed my dad! We eventually had to go to the hospital so he could get some stitches. We laughed about it later and we all agreed that he probably couldn't catch me anymore."

Byrd was the 4th-round selection of the Cleveland Indians in the June 1991 draft. He was traded to the New York Mets in 1995 and made his big-league debut on July 28 of that year. "My wife and parents missed my first game," Byrd acknowledged, "but I'll tell you what they did do. The next series we played in Cincinnati and they were able to see me play there. I was with the Mets and I remember striking out Barry Larkin on a 3–2 fastball away. It was at that moment I felt as though I made it to the big leagues."

Byrd played with seven different major-league teams during his career, which required a lot of moving around that was not necessarily conducive to a stable upbringing for his children. It may help explain why Byrd's main concern is raising his sons with the same love his father bestowed on him. Byrd explained: "The Bible says, 'Love covers a multitude of sins' and I knew I was going to make mistakes when I became a parent. But the one thing I want my kids to feel is love. I want that love to help erase and cover the mistakes I may make as a parent, so that is why I try to spend as much time as I can with my kids. I have two sons," Byrd added. "My oldest is a big-time athlete and he loves baseball and my youngest is not, so we do Cub Scouts together and we do stuff he wants to do. I like to spend time with them and I try to wear many hats."

Just as Byrd is proud of his two sons, his dad is proud of him. "It just goes with the territory," Byrd said matter-of-factly. "I've also been very fortunate to have as many years in this game as I have. I often tell people, that I'm not good enough to stay with one team and not bad enough to retire!"

♦ FRANK CATALANOTTO ♦

Frank Catalanotto grew up in Smithtown, a town on the North Shore of Long Island in New York. "I grew up a Yankees fan," said the well-rounded athlete. "My favorites were Reggie Jackson and Don Mattingly. In fact, I recently got to meet Mattingly and it was pretty neat meeting my idol. That was a special moment for me."

It is special to meet someone you idolize, but many times the person you really idolize is right under your nose (or over your head) and guiding your way through the sport you love.

"My father was my coach all throughout Little League. He was either the head coach or assistant coach. He was always there. He coached, worked the concession stand, he was a taxi driver for the team, he did a little bit of everything."

Catalanotto appreciated his father's contributions after the games as well. "I remember driving home from games and no matter how well or not I did in the game, my dad was never hard on me. He was always supportive. He never had a negative thing to say. I remember having a bad game when I was very young and I was very upset. My dad just said to me, 'Hey, keep your head up. Take this opportunity and learn from what just happened. Learn from your mistakes so you can be better at it.' Even today, I still think about that moment when things don't go right. I look to the positive from it and, in my dad's words, learn from what just happened. I think about how I can improve upon it. And that isn't something that just applies to lessons on the field but it is something that pertains to everything you do in life."

Catalanotto graduated from Smithtown East High School in 1992. He played soccer and ran track, but excelled in baseball—enough to be selected by the Detroit Tigers in the 10th round of the June draft that year.

After bopping around in the minors for five years, he was called up in September 1997 and made his major-league debut as a pinch hitter on September 3 at Atlanta. He made his first major-league start—at second base (one of the numerous positions he would play in the majors)—on September 7 against Anaheim.

"It was in Detroit," Catalanotto recalled about his first start and the first MLB game his father saw him play. "I was so nervous and scared. It was my first big-league game. It was a great moment for me and I was so happy he was there."

Catalanotto has gone on to play for over thirteen years in the majors. "My dad is the proudest father ever and it's great," he admitted. "He's my biggest cheerleader and that's no lie. I'm from New York and it is definitely a special moment when I get back home and play in Yankee Stadium. My parents actually live five minutes from my house and he is always handing out photos and baseball cards of me to everyone. He is very proud!"

Catalanotto's dad is also a reliable source for advice. "Whenever there is an issue that comes up in life, I'm on the phone with him," revealed Catalanotto. "He is a very smart man. Whenever I have a question I don't know, I call my dad, He watches every single game. So when things are going bad, I'll talk to him and he gives me some advice. Whether I take it or not, it's good to know he's watching and he is there for me. He's my guardian angel!"

Joba Chamberlain made his major-league debut on August 7, 2007, with the New York Yankees in Toronto, but his road to the big leagues began on a rough path.

Chamberlain's father, Harlan, was born on the Winnebago Indian reservation, but he was taken off the reservation at a young age to be treated for polio. The polio left him deaf in his left ear and with weakness in his left arm and leg. The father of two uses a scooter to get around, but the scooter and the arm weakness never stopped Harlan from coaching and playing catch with his son.

Originally named Justin, Joba was a chubby child, not very tall and not very fast, but he would play catch with his father regularly. If he missed his father's glove, he would have to retrieve the baseball due to his father's limited mobility, so his aim became very good.

"It was good having my dad play catch with me every day growing up. And it was a great motivator for me," said Chamberlain. "He played catch with me all the time. And now I get to take care of him and that is awesome."

Harlan, a single father, taught his daughter and son by example; he was loud, but considerate of everyone and enthusiastic about life. He made sure his children learned about their American Indian roots and stayed in touch with his relatives. He taught them about working hard and never giving up. But most of all, he encouraged them to do their best. "My dad always stressed to me to be myself," Chamberlain said. "You don't always have to be the best ballplayer out there, but you have to try your best and always be prepared for what life throws at you."

Chamberlain did not start pitching until his senior year at Northeast High School in his hometown of Lincoln, Nebraska. He struck out 29 in 31.1 innings in his senior year and garnered second-team Super State honors from Lincoln's *Journal Star*. But he was not drafted, nor did he immediately attend college. Joba instead helped to pay the family's bills by working briefly for the City of Lincoln's maintenance department.

For his freshman year, the right-hander went to the University of Nebraska at Kearney, a Division II school. It was there that he began working harder to get his body in shape. Chamberlain transferred to the University of Nebraska the following year and helped the Cornhuskers reach the 2005 College World Series, as he posted a 10–2 record and a 2.81 ERA. In fact, he helped them to their first College World Series win.

Suddenly, Chamberlain's path to the big leagues became much clearer. Despite suffering through a bout of triceps tendinitis in 2006, Chamberlain was selected by the Yankees with a supplemental pick as the 41st overall selection in the first round of the June draft. He did not pitch in the minors in 2006, but he did pitch in the Hawaiian winter league.

He began the 2007 season as a starter for the Tampa Yankees (A) in the Florida State League. He was progressing through the minor leagues with the Trenton Thunder (AA) and Scranton/Wilkes-Barre Red Barons (AAA), when he was moved to the bullpen in late July. One week later, he made his major-league debut, culminating his impressive progression through four levels of the Yankees organization in a single season.

Harlan Chamberlain's health prevented him from attending his son's debut, but he did make the three-hour car ride to Kansas City to see his son pitch in the Yankees-Royals series that ran September 7–9. When the Yankees won the World Series two years later in 2009, Harlan was there again to see his son pitch.

"I told my son for years that he would do this, we would talk about getting to the World Series all the time" said Harlan in Yankee Stadium. "We just shared that moment while realizing that he did it. I pinched myself a few times. It's pretty awesome.

"We love each other very much. This whole adventure in life is about family, and, in our case, it's about father and son."

That strong relationship between father and son continues to this day. "I talk to my dad on a daily basis," said Chamberlain. "I don't always ask him for advice, but we talk all of the time. I can't ask for anything more. He has always been there for me!"

◆ TONY CLARK ◆

Tony Clark was born in Kansas, but grew up in the San Diego area. "My dad was my coach in my first year of kid-pitch and he was also my coach when I turned twelve years old," said Clark, a fifteen-year major leaguer.

"My dad taught me about hard work," stated Clark. "He was always one of those guys that believed in that. Because he was the coach, I was always the first to get to the field and the last one to leave practice and games. It is actually a policy that I have adopted today with my job here. I try to be the first player in the clubhouse and the last one to leave . . . and the work I put in between has always paid off."

Clark retains plenty of good memories, as well as good habits, from his childhood. "My most memorable game from my childhood was from my twelve-year-old league when I was in the All-Star game. I was already in my second year of switch-hitting and I hit a walk-off home run to win the All-Star game. And, I remember," he added with a big smile, "after the game my reward was a trip to McDonald's and getting a Happy Meal. To me that was a big reward and that was the most vivid memory growing up."

The six foot seven first baseman is a 1990 graduate of Christian High School. "I grew up in San Diego, but I was born in the Midwest," said Clark. "For some reason, though, my favorite team growing up was the Yankees. I believe every player should play at least one year for the Yankees.

"I got to play for the Yankees for one year," Clark recalled of his 2004 season. "It was a great opportunity to put on the pinstripes. Being a Yankees fan growing up, it was exciting. Again, I wish every player had at least one opportunity to feel what it's like to put on the pinstripes, even for just a little while."

Clark revealed that he had an individual player, as well as a team, he esteemed above all others in baseball. "Ironically enough, our Little League teams once in awhile would have baseball cards made for the players. I remember the one I had made when I was ten years old. We had to list our favorite team and favorite baseball hero. My baseball hero was Hank Aaron. Now, growing up and being in this game, I had the opportunity to learn and appreciate more about Hank Aaron. I got the chance to get his autograph and was greatly impressed by the character of this man and the magnitude [of the impact] he had on this game."

◆ AARON COOK ◆

Aaron Cook grew up in Ohio, and not surprisingly, he was a Cincinnati Reds fan. "I used to follow Bench and Rose, and when I got older and when those guys got out of the game, my favorite was then Barry Larkin. When I was little I used to wear his No. 11 on my uniform," Cook remembered fondly.

Cook's father played a big part in his baseball life. "From as young as I can remember until I was about fifteen years old, my dad had been my coach," said Cook. "From the point I picked up a bat and a baseball, my dad took on the job of coaching his son. My dad loved baseball. He played the game himself, for an Army traveling team. So it was only natural for me to play it, too."

Cook shared the most impactful advice he got from his father. "My dad taught me that if you are going to do something, then do it with all your heart," he said. "He never forced me to play sports, but told me if I'm going to commit to a sport then I had to stick it out. It was the main lesson I learned from my dad."

The right-handed pitcher stuck with baseball and was selected by the Colorado Rockies in the 2nd round of the June 1997 draft out of Hamilton High School. Cook's major-league debut arrived on August 10, 2002, when he pitched in relief against the Chicago Cubs.

"The great part of that day was that I got called up to the big leagues on my dad's birthday," recalled Cook. "It was definitely a great birthday gift. I didn't even have to buy anything for him that year! It will always be a great memory for both of us. It was a lot of fun that first time in the big leagues."

◆ COCO CRISP ◆

Covelli Loyce Crisp was originally called "Co" by his great grandmother when he was young. His sister and god-brother lengthened the name to "Coco" in honor of the character on the cereal box of Cocoa Krispies. But the name didn't really stick . . . until years later.

In 2002, Covelli's professional team-mates heard of his childhood nickname and liked it. . . . He's been Coco ever since.

In his "Covelli" days, his father was his coach. "He was my coach beginning in Little League and continuing through when I was twelve years old," Crisp said.

"I remember when I hit my first home run over the big, high fence with a tennis ball. I was actually playing a game of base-ball with my cousins when we went up to visit them during summer vacation. I must have been in elementary school. It was almost like the movie *The Sandlot*, when I couldn't get the tennis ball back," Crisp said with a smile. "I remember thinking to myself how powerful I was to hit a ball that far. I even made a bet with my father—for each home run I'd hit, I'd get a new Nintendo game. I think I got six games that year. He didn't make the bet afterwards."

A native of Los Angeles, California, Crisp graduated from Inglewood High School and attended Pierce Junior College before being selected by the St. Louis Cardinals in the 7th round of the June 1999 draft. After being re-dubbed "Coco" by team-mates in the Cardinals minor-league system, he was traded to the Cleveland Indians on August 7, 2002, and made his Major League Baseball debut eight days later, on August 15, against the Tamp Bay Devil Rays.

"My first game was in Tampa when I was with Cleveland," he recalled. "Then we went to Anaheim to play the Angels and that is where my parents got to see me. It was *close* to my debut. It was nice because I was able to go to them, being from that area, and they didn't have to make the long trip."

The speedy outfielder remains in touch with his father, who is still coaching him. "I just got an e-mail from him about hitting. I was reading it and he wanted to remind me to put my front foot down more, turn, step soft, put your hands this way, and do this and that," Crisp shared with a laugh.

Crisp summarized his relationship with his father. "All I know is that he is always there for me."

◆ BUBBA CROSBY ◆

Richard Steven Crosby grew up in Texas and played in the major leagues from 2003 through 2006 for the Los Angeles Dodgers and New York Yankees. Name doesn't ring a bell? Before you reach for your favorite baseball reference guide, consider that you may know him by his more commonly heard name—Bubba.

Crosby's fifteen-month-old sister, Charmin, was responsible for the nickname. She couldn't say "brother" and her version of the word stuck as his name.

"Almost everyone in Texas is Bubba when you are growing up," said Crosby, who tried to call himself Rick or Rickey in school. But when friends called the house asking for him, no one knew whom they were talking about.

His parents may not have been familiar with his childhood alias, but they were always around for their kids. "My dad was pretty much my coach all the way up until I got too old and he couldn't be my coach anymore," said Crosby. "It was probably up to senior high that he was my coach. I just remember him always there."

He was certainly there for one of Crosby's favorite baseball memories. "I was in a machine-pitch league and I hit a home run," Crosby recounted. "At the start of the inning we were down quite a few runs and we came back and the home run I hit got us the victory. When I was rounding third base I could see my dad and my teammates waiting for me at home plate. I jumped on home plate and then into my dad's arms. It was a real sentimental moment for me and my dad."

After graduating from Bellaire High School, Crosby went to Rice University. It was there that he switched from pitching to playing outfield with teammate Lance Berkman. His success at Rice got him selected in the first round (23rd overall) of the June 1998 draft by the Dodgers.

He didn't make his major-league debut until May 29, 2003, in Colorado. "My first start was with the Dodgers, but I wasn't there long," stated Crosby. He was traded to the Yankees organization on July 31, 2003. "The first opportunity my mom and dad got to see me in uniform was in Texas. They were both there in hopes to see me play against the Rangers, but I didn't play there either. And then, finally, they traveled to New York and got to see me play against the Boston Red Sox.

"I remember hitting this triple," Crosby continued, "and I got up after the slide and tried to look for them in the stands. I knew the section, but everyone was standing up and cheering. New York fans love triples. I knew he was there with a big smile on his face. I may not have actually heard what he was saying at that very moment, but in my heart I knew exactly what he was saying."

Crosby had shoulder surgery in 2007 and was unable to pass a physical in 2008, resulting in his retirement from professional baseball. But throughout his career and his life, he has turned to his dad for advice. "My dad is the first person I still call to this day," noted Crosby. "He'll be the first to admit this level is a little more advanced for him to help me with, but even today, I can still turn to him when I feel lost at the plate. It's more comforting than anything else. I know he's watching and I know he's feeling for me, too. When I struggle, he struggles, too. It's nice to just talk to him and hear his input and his fatherly advice."

The greatest piece of fatherly advice he received was to practice loyalty and honesty, on and off the field. "Everyone deserves and wants an honest answer," Crosby explained. "They may not want to hear it or even like it, but you will eventually be respected for it."

◆ JOSE CRUZ JR. ◆

Jose Cruz had a nineteen-year Major League Baseball career spanning from 1970 to 1988 with the St. Louis Cardinals, Houston Astros, and New York Yankees. He spent another thirteen years (1997–2009) as a coach for the Astros. But his most important job came immediately after he retired as a player in 1988, when he coached his son Jose Jr.

"My father had an extensive baseball career and it wasn't until my freshman year of high school—when he was in his first year of retirement from the game—that he actually had the chance to coach me," recalled Jose Jr. "I think I was a good outlet for him once he left the game. So he was able to use that energy and coach me . . . it worked out great for the two of us. We worked on baseball all of the time."

It is not surprising that so many of Jose Jr.'s memories revolve around the ballpark. "Baseball has always been a part of my life . . . it couldn't be helped," he stated. "I have so many memories. I remember one time getting knocked out during the Caribbean World Series by a foul ball, literally knocked out, when I was just five years old. Later, I even got to see my dad's last hit in the big leagues. It was a grand slam. It was a great way to end a career. For me, these are the memories I have of him that stand out."

Born in Puerto Rico, but raised in Texas, Jose Jr. went to Bellaire High School and helped his team get ranked No. 1 by *USA Today* in 1992, his senior year. The Atlanta Braves selected him in the fifteenth round, but the outfielder opted to go to Rice University.

He was selected by the Seattle Mariners in the first round (3rd overall) in the June 1995 draft. He made his major-league debut just a short time later, on May 31, 1997.

"My dad has always been my biggest fan and biggest critic," chuckled Jose Jr., "but I still turn to him for advice all the time."

And the greatest advice he received from his father? "With baseball he was always big on hustling when you are out there. No matter what, you've got to hustle," said Jose Jr. "He also taught me to have fun with the game and enjoy what you are doing. He would often say that people lose sight of that. Even to this day he still stresses that fact—to enjoy what you are doing."

◆ MICHAEL CUDDYER ◆

Many major leaguers get off to a slow start with their professional baseball careers. For Michael Cuddyer that slow start came even before his Little League career got going.

"It was right before my first organized game," Cuddyer explained. "I was playing kickball in the street with my family and friends and I was so excited that this upcoming Saturday I was going to play in my first game. This had to be the Tuesday or Wednesday prior to that game. Someone kicked the ball and I went to catch it and ended up breaking my thumb. For the next six weeks I wasn't able to play, and being just six years old, it was tearing me apart. I guess you can say it was my first time on the disabled list!"

Cuddyer did eventually get to play Little League and his father, Henry, was by his side. "My dad was my coach in Little League and then he was my coach all the way up until right before high school," said the six foot two infielder and outfielder. "And today, he is still my best cheerleader! He has always kept up with everything I'm doing."

Cuddyer went to Great Bridge High School in Virginia. In 1997, his senior year, he was honored as Virginia Player of the Year and Gatorade Player of the Year, and named to the *USA Today* All-Star team. And, to top it off, he was selected by the Minnesota Twins in the first round (9th overall) of the June draft.

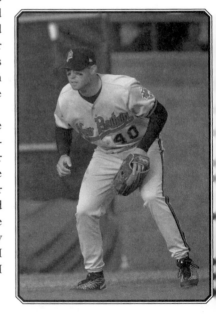

He rose quickly through the minors and had his contract purchased by the Twins on September 18, 2001. He made his major-league debut a few days later, on September 23 against Cleveland as a designated hitter. "My dad actually got to see me because he came up for my second series," said Cuddyer. "I didn't play in that first series, but I did get to play in that second series and he was there to be a part of it!"

Through it all, Cuddyer said the greatest lesson he learned from his father remains with him. "Hands down," Cuddyer said emphatically, "the greatest thing he taught me was what the work ethic meant. He always led by example. He was a distributor for Little Debbie cakes and each day he would get up very early to do his job. He definitely taught me the importance of the work ethic."

Cuddyer is currently a member of the Colorado Rockies.

◆ JACK CUST ◆

Jack Cust grew up in Flemington, New Jersey, and, like many kids from that area, he grew up liking the New York Yankees. "My first and fondest memory growing up was going to Yankee Stadium with my dad and watching the game," recalled Cust. "Going to Yankee Stadium and taking in that experience for a kid that grew up in New Jersey and following the Yankees all my life was the most memorable part of growing up for me. It helped inspire me knowing that I wanted to be a major-league ballplayer when I grew up."

The Yankee wannabe had a father with a great baseball plan for his son. "My dad was my coach all the way up to high school. Yet, he still played a big part in my high school teams," said Cust. "My dad was probably the most important coach that I had and for a lot of kids he ended up coaching! He basically taught me everything I needed to prepare for life."

Cust went to Immaculata High School in Flemington and, following his senior year in 1997, was selected in the first round (30th overall) of the June draft by the Arizona Diamondbacks. That same year, he and his father founded the Jack Cust Baseball Academy, now known as Diamond Nation.

Cust went on to make his major-league debut on September 26, 2001, against the Milwaukee Brewers. He has played for six major league teams, as a designated hitter and as an outfielder. "It never ends for me and my dad," said Cust. "I still turn to him for advice. Maybe not as much today regarding baseball . . . because these days he sometimes has too much to say. But he has changed and has learned. Today, my dad is more of a psychological coach for me and for those questions concerning my personal life."

Cust tries to pass on what he learned from his father to young players. "What I want to tell Little Leaguers is to work hard and never forget to have fun with the game. Always enjoy it and never take the game too seriously. I always knew I wanted to be a ballplayer and even though I played other sports, this sport kind of chose me."

◆ MARK DEROSA ◆

Like many other boys across the country, Mark DeRosa grew up loving sports. He is an example of how hard work and talent pays off, but it all goes back to his childhood.

"I remember being in wonder of my older brother and his friends," recalled DeRosa. "It was just one of those things. I always wanted to be around him and follow him and wanted to play with the older kids. No matter whether it was football, baseball, or basketball my brother always included me in the things he did. That is one of my fondest memories."

DeRosa grew up in Passaic, New Jersey. His father coached him from T-ball until he was twelve years old. "My dad taught me the fundamentals of the game. He taught me to have fun and he taught me how to win. I'll tell you what, that combination is one of the toughest things to teach. He never let me forget to go out there and have fun. That is what it is all about, having fun, and enjoying the game. But my dad also taught me how to be competitive and remind me that it is nice to win, too, and some championships along the way are good. They are the memories you keep. He'd say, 'Guys, have fun out there, but it's okay to go out there and try to win as well.'"

DeRosa reminisced, "When I got to play baseball, and I got my first uniform, and got to pick my uniform number, and opening day ceremonies, that parade through town—they were all wonderful memories. So was being around my buddies after the game, getting a snow cone or hitting a home run during the game and then getting a pint of ice cream because of the big hit. I know a lot of things haven't changed for many kids even today."

A graduate of Bergen Catholic High School where he earned All-State honors in baseball and football, DeRosa went on to the Wharton School at the University of Pennsylvania where he quarterbacked the football team (1993–95) and played varsity baseball (1994–96). He was selected by the Atlanta Braves in the 7th round of the June draft in 1996, and began his professional career, but he did get to complete his business degree in 1997.

DeRosa made his major-league debut just two years after being drafted in 1998. His ability to play many positions has made him a desirable player throughout his career. He has played for the Braves, Texas Rangers, Chicago Cubs, Cleveland Indians, St. Louis Cardinals, San Francisco Giants, and Washington Nationals . . . and his father has followed him through it all.

"We are kind of best friends," said DeRosa of his father. "I talk with him at least three to four times a week. He tries to help me out from what he catches of my play on television. He's more my mental coach than anything else. He's someone that has helped me stay grounded. This game is so mental to begin with and you have those coaches who try to help, but my dad always wants to keep things on a positive note even when things go bad.

"My dad is also a realist," he continued. "He tells it like it is. For example, when I ground out to third three times in a game, he'd say, 'What are you doing that for? Don't you know how this guy is going to pitch you? What did I always teach you? I taught you better!'"

It all goes back to his youth. "I remember me and a few guys from the team drove by a Little League field while a game was going on and we stopped by to watch. Nothing really has changed much even after all this time. You watch those Little League guys and you think to yourself, 'That was me way back then.'"

◆ MATT DIAZ ◆

Every player in this book has had his father as his coach at some point in his life. Not too many, however, have had him as his coach for seventeen years, like Matt Diaz did.

It all began in 1981. "I was a batboy on my older brother's T-ball team," the very likable Diaz recalled of the T-ball team his father coached. "When one of the players quit, I was there to take his place. So my dad pulled me from my job as batboy and I started playing. I was only three years old," Diaz said with a smile. "That was the start of my dad coaching me. He continued coaching me all the way through high school, until the age of nineteen."

In addition to coaching, the elder Diaz was involved in Baseball Ministries, which serviced the religious and spiritual needs of players throughout the game. His godfather is former Detroit Tigers catcher, Matt Nokes. It only seemed logical that baseball was destined to be a big part of Matt Diaz's life.

"I led the eleven- to twelve-year-old league in home runs and was feeling pretty good about my accomplishment," Diaz recalled. "My father said to me, 'That was fun, now I think it is time for you to start learning how to hit.'" Diaz admitted to being confused by the statement, but looking back the advice made perfect sense. Basically, his father wanted him to start thinking about hitting the ball the other way, using all aspects of the field.

More advice Diaz received from his father and other coaches came through a simple phrase that was uttered often, "Don't be average!" He confessed this was the best piece of advice he ever got, and has applied it to aspects of his life beyond just the game of baseball.

"If you are going to do something, either be really terrible at it or be great at it, because no one remembers the average guy," Diaz explained. "This is why I have stuck around pro ball as long as I have—baseball is what I want to do."

Diaz attended Florida State University. His father was not his coach there, but still followed him as much as he could. "When I was in college my dad would call into the radio station that carried the game and listen in," Diaz explained. "He called me after one game when I went hitless and told me that my hands sounded low. I said, 'Come on! You can't tell my hands were low!'"

Despite his disbelief, Diaz went back and looked at film of the game and admitted his hands were indeed low. So he asked his father how he knew his hands were low. His father based his assumption on the number of pitches his son had fouled back and the location of the foul balls. "Fathers really do know best," Diaz said with a smile and a shake of his head. And, I guess former President Gerald Ford was right when he, too, said, "I watch a lot of baseball on radio."

Diaz was selected by the Tampa Bay Devil Rays in the 17th round of the June 1999 draft. He made it to the majors for a few at-bats in 2003 and 2004. He was a back-up player for the Kansas City Royals in 2005 and finally came into his own with the Atlanta Braves in 2006.

His father still follows his progress. "I don't have to turn to him for advice," said Diaz with a chuckle. "Meaning, I get phone messages from him after games, especially those he sees on the television, all the time. The advice is always there for me!"

◆ SCOTT DOHMANN ◆

Pitcher Scott Dohmann grew up in the South, but in his early years he was not thinking about pitching. "I will always remember this little ballpark in Carolyn Park, New Orleans, where I grew up. I guess it was because of the home runs I used to hit there," he recalled. "I hit a few during my Little League days . . . unlike later when the better pitchers caught up to me and my hitting," he added with a grin.

"Maybe it was because my dad was pitching to me then. My dad was funny, when I'd hit a home run off him, he'd get so excited; he'd jump up and down. And I remember the whole team would line up at home plate giving me high fives," recalled Dohmann.

"He was my coach through coach-pitch ball. My dad pitched to us and that helped me out refining my swing as a batter. I felt more confident with him pitching to me than anyone else. I knew my dad and how he'd pitch to me. He concentrated very hard to make sure I'd get a good pitch to hit. He knew I liked the ball high."

The six foot one reliever said his father gave him more than just a steady diet of high fastballs. "I remember my dad would make me grits and scrambled eggs before every Little League game. He mixed them up for me, but I didn't always like them," Dohmann confessed. "I hated them, in fact, but he told me if I ate them I'd be big and strong and then I'd hit a home run that day. He'd call it my 'home run breakfast.'

"I still don't like them at all," Dohmann continued, "but every once in awhile, I'll turn back the clock and have some. The fact that he'd say I would hit a home run—I was willing to sacrifice my taste buds. Little did I know that he was just trying to ensure that I'd have a good breakfast. I just didn't know any better back then. I just thought he wanted me to hit a home run."

Beyond throwing high balls for home runs and cooking a breakfast for heroes, Dohmann's father had a lot of lessons to teach his son. "Overall, he taught me how to play the game the right way and live life the right way, treating people with respect," said Dohmann. "I guess he taught me how to be a team player, knowing that you are not bigger than anyone else and that this game will go on with or without you. My dad taught me that keeping the faith was so important and that everything happens for a reason. He taught me to be able to accept the good with the bad, and know that this is all happening for a reason, and not just being happy when the good comes around. He stressed for me to enjoy and embrace whatever comes your way."

Dohmann attended the University of Louisiana at Lafayette and pitched in the 2000 College World Series. That same month, he was selected by the Colorado Rockies in the 6th round of the June draft.

On June 15, 2004, he was called up to the majors and made his major-league debut that night. "My debut was in Denver," said Dohmann, "my dad, my mom, my sister, and grandma all went. My sister told me when my dad saw that big-league field for the first time he broke down and cried. She never saw him do that in the past and to me that still hits me right here," he said pounding his heart. "She said that he almost went down to his knees with joy. He was truly overcome by the experience and to me that will always be pretty special."

Dohmann still regularly talks with his dad. "He calls me after every game I pitch," Dohmann revealed. "He follows the game and my career religiously. I'll admit there are some games I don't want to talk about and some games I do. I know he doesn't brag about his son being a major leaguer, but deep inside I know he is just bubbling with pride."

The very likable Dohmann shared a final thought. "I was always a fan of baseball. I can't say I had any one idol, but I always looked up to my dad."

◆ CHRIS DUFFY ◆

"My dad was not just my coach, he was also president of our Little League program," bragged Chris Duffy, outfielder for the Pittsburgh Pirates and Milwaukee Brewers. "So I was fortunate to spend all day and all night at the ball fields. Even when I didn't have a game, there was some game going on and I was there with my dad. At times, I spent seven days a week at the field. I helped my dad with everything, from working on the field to umpiring a game."

Thinking back on all the time he has spent in baseball, Duffy recalled a lesson his father taught him that has helped carry him through it all. "Probably the one thing that I learned from my dad that continues today was to always play with passion and stay competitive," said a thoughtful Duffy. "That has definitely helped me to get as far as I have.

"I'm not what you call a tooled player. I can't hit a ball five hundred feet or throw a ball ninety-five miles per hour. What got me here is being competitive and the passion I have for the game. And this is what my dad was able to instill in me at a very early age," said Duffy.

"My dad was a big baseball guy. I remember pictures of me as a baby holding a Wiffle bat. But if I had to pick one story, I remember when I was growing up I started out as a right-handed batter. One day during a Little League game I came up with the bases loaded and my dad wanted me to hit left-handed for the first time! I remember coming up to bat and being upset, but my dad felt I would be better from the left side of the plate. Today, I am a predominately left-handed hitter. That one defining moment helped to change my life."

His professional career almost began in 2000 when he was drafted by the Boston Red Sox in the 43rd round out of South Mountain Community College. Instead, Duffy opted to go to Arizona State University. The following year, he was selected by the Pirates in the eighth round of the June draft and his pro career officially began.

"My dad was at my big-league debut in 2005 against the Padres," said a proud Duffy of his MLB debut on April 7 with the Pirates in San Diego. "It was a special experience for me. My folks never got the opportunity to see me play when I was in the minor leagues. But I grew up in Arizona, so it wasn't too far for them to travel when I was in San Diego. So they were able to come to the game and that was pretty neat for me."

The energetic outfielder still reaches out to his father. "My dad likes to stay in the loop," he explained. "He wants to know what's going on. It's not as much technical or physical for him anymore, but he can watch a game and he knows if I am playing 'with that fire,' as he likes to put it. When he thinks that I am not playing to that level, he is always there to bring it to my attention. He is definitely a great motivator to me."

◆ MORGAN ENSBERG ◆

Strangely enough, some major-league players didn't dream of playing baseball when they were kids. Morgan Ensberg was one of those kids.

"I didn't plan on being a professional baseball player at all," Ensberg confessed. "I didn't even dream about being a professional player. I thought that I would go to school, end up going to college and then go to work in a bank just like my dad. I always thought he was a great role model, so I thought I would follow him, figuring he was doing things right."

Ensberg grew up near Los Angeles and graduated from Redondo Union High School. "Growing up in Southern California was pretty special. You didn't just play baseball, you played everything," Ensberg recalled. "I grew up a Dodgers and Lakers fan, but we spent a lot of time around the beach and playing in the park. My dad was very involved—he coached me in baseball, soccer, and basketball."

Ensberg's father coached him in sports, but the biggest lessons he learned from him were not sports-related. "I learned much more off the field than on it from my dad," Ensberg admitted. "Most important, he taught me how to be a man and how to be a God-fearing man. He is a Christian man who goes to work, provides for his family, puts his head down, and doesn't complain, and I was able to learn this all from a guy who just knows how to do it right. There were five of us in our family, and he was especially big on education and very much about school being number one."

Ensberg went on to USC after high school and was the third baseman for the USC team that became national champions in 1998. He was selected by the Houston Astros that year in the 9th round of the June draft and made his major-league debut as a pinch-hitter for the Astros on September 20, 2000, in St. Louis. "My dad and mom came to see me play when I got called up in 2000," he recalled with pride. "They were both there to see me play in my first game."

True to the lessons his father taught, it is not surprising to learn that his parents are proud of him, but not blown away with the "glamorous side of baseball."

"My dad is not too impressed with the whole baseball thing," Ensberg stated. "I think they [his parents] are happier with the path it takes, the hard work that it takes and not just being lucky or the timing issue. I think they are most proud of the fact that I appeared to reach my final goal of being a big leaguer. So again, he's most proud of—nothing to do with the sport—me and the hard work involved and how you eventually handle the failure when you are faced with it."

After a nine-year major-league career with Houston, the San Diego Padres, and the New York Yankees, Ensberg retired and is living in California with his wife and three children. "I talk to my dad quite a bit still to this day," said Ensberg. "When I have questions, he is definitely one of the first people I go to."

◆ SCOTT ERICKSON ◆

For Scott Erickson, growing up around baseball was a way of life.

"I grew up and played baseball all of my life and my dad was a big sports guy," recalled Erickson. "I remember going to his fast-pitch softball games. I know he played sports in high school and college. I remember we went to baseball games and football games all the time."

The right-handed pitcher from Long Beach, California, also remembered the first game he attended with his dad. "My very first game I went to was at Candlestick Park and I watched the Giants play," stated Erickson.

"My dad was my coach up until I was about ten years old," Erickson continued. "As long as I can remember, I played baseball and my dad was always out there throwing the ball to me."

The fifteen-year MLB veteran confessed he was a baseball junkie. "I was always a huge baseball fan. . . . Pete Rose was one of my favorites. I also liked Mike Schmidt and Steve Carlton. I followed the Big Red Machine and I liked the Oakland A's. There were tons of other guys I remember watching as I was growing up," Erickson recalled.

"*Monday Night Baseball* was my very favorite television show in the world. It was a lucky night when I was a kid and could sit there with my dad and watch the game."

◆ JOHNNY ESTRADA ◆

Catcher Johnny Estrada grew up in Northern California where his father coached him nearly every step of the way in his early baseball career. "My dad was my coach all through Little League. He was my coach in Babe Ruth ball. He was even my hitting coach my last two years of high school baseball. My dad was there beginning at age five and all through my years growing up with baseball," recalled Estrada.

"My dad was also the one who taught me to switch-hit, and that was probably the best thing he had ever done for me. I remember hating him for it back then, taking all those 0 for 4s while batting left-handed. He convinced me to stick with it. I remember he'd be down at third base coaching and telling me after I'd try and bat right-handed to switch. He'd whistle down at me to turn around and get in the left-handed batter's box. And, I'd be pouting and after the game I would cry and say, 'I can't hit left-handed' and stuff like that. But he made me stick to it and that helped.

"My dad always provided me with the tools to play baseball on a daily basis growing up. I soon developed better hand-to-hand coordination and got better and better every day. Before, I used to curse my dad for making me bat left-handed, but today every time I have to bat from that side of the plate, I say, 'Thank you!'"

The affable 2004 All-Star admitted that he made it to the majors because of his father. "My dad taught me perseverance and the concept of hard work," said Estrada. "Ultimately, one of the main reasons why I made it to the big leagues was because I was a catcher, and better yet, a switch-hitting catcher. It was a great commodity and my dad taught me way back then that would be a good avenue for me to take in order for me to reach my dreams. My dad knew I wasn't going to be the fastest, strongest, or biggest kid on the field. I was short and chunky, but I could catch and I could hit.

Estrada's father would still love to coach him, but "there came a point in my career that I had to make a separation with my dad as my coach," admitted Estrada. "Coming up in the minor leagues, he wasn't able to be there on a daily basis to see me play and coach me.

"My dad still loves to talk hitting with me at times, but it's different," Estrada continued. "I kind of took my game to the next level and he wasn't able to be there and assist me in what I had to learn. But my dad still leaves me messages on my phone like, 'Hey, your swing is long!' or 'Your elbow is all wrong!' or 'You're trying to pull the ball!' or my favorite, 'You're over-striding!' I'd call him back and tell him, 'Dad, I've got coaches here that have played in the big leagues!' Then my wife would call him back and say, 'Dad, you've got to stop getting in his head.' Over the years he has tuned it down somewhat and he has become more of a fan."

Looking back, Estrada recalled his first memories of the game. "I can remember my dad used to play semipro baseball when I was really small. I think I was four years old," the father of three shared. "He was a player-manager and I used to be the batboy. I used to put on a helmet and think to myself, 'What a stud I am putting this helmet on.' I remember imagining myself batting and playing on the team. I thought I was one of the players. Then after the game, I used to hang out with the boys and I felt like I was one of the guys. I loved just being around the game."

Estrada also fondly recalls his memories of his early exposure to major-league players. "I was a die-hard Oakland A's fan growing up," he revealed. "I remember taking BART [Bay Area Rapid Transit] to the stadium with my dad and we used to sit up in the bleachers. We always went to Opening Day. I remember watching the Bash Brothers [Jose Canseco and Mark McGwire] and there was Rickey Henderson. We had some good years in Oakland and I got to experience some championships. But I can still remember it like it was yesterday, when Kirk Gibson came up and hit *that* home run off Dennis Eckersley. Even today, I still hate watching that highlight."

After graduating from Roosevelt High School and attending the College of the Sequoias Junior College, Estrada was selected by the Philadelphia Phillies in the 17th round of the June 1997 draft.

Estrada was called up just shy of four years later and made his Major League Baseball debut on May 15, 2001, against the Milwaukee Brewers. "It was at Veterans Stadium and I was playing for the Phillies. I remember thinking to myself that day how it kind of all came together for me. All of the hard work was paying off. I was reaching my dreams. But there were a lot of emotions for me on that day, some butterflies, and there was a lot of nervousness. I felt like I needed to pinch myself and would ask myself, 'Is this really happening?' he recalled.

"You spend your whole life trying to reach your dreams and you are never really prepared how to react when you achieve them—when you reach something you've been dreaming about all of your life, and now it's your job and your livelihood. Every so often you have to stand back and say to yourself, 'This is a kid's dream that I am living and how lucky I am!'"

◆ KYLE FARNSWORTH ◆

When you are a kid, your parents seem like superheroes—they are everywhere, doing everything for their children. That seems to be how Kyle Farnsworth felt about his father.

"I can always remember my dad doing what dads do. He was my coach, on and off, throughout Little League, but he was always there doing just about everything," recalled Farnsworth.

"He always told me never to give up, no matter what. He'd say, 'Go out and do your best and that is all that you can ever do.'"
His father Lynn never gave up either.

"My dad was a fighter pilot in Vietnam who flew F-4 and F-100 bombers. He was shot down twice, and I know I might not have been here if there had been different," a very emotional Farnsworth shared as he placed a hand on the shoulder of his son, Stone. "It was really a close call for him. After he was shot down, he could even hear the chatter of the enemy, talking all around him and knowing that they were looking for him. He doesn't like to talk about it. All I know is that if they found him, I wouldn't have been here today, and nor would my son. I even have a tattoo of a F-100 on my shoulder to commemorate his flying days."

Farnsworth went on to study at Abraham Baldwin Agricultural College in Georgia. But he also followed his father's advice and never gave up, continuing to pursue his dream of playing professional baseball until it led to him getting selected by the Chicago Cubs in the 47th round of the June 1994 draft. He made his Major League Baseball debut less than five years later on April 29, 1999. He is currently with the Tampa Bay Rays.

"My dad still calls me and we talk about pitching and my mechanics," Farnsworth shared. "That is a good thing because that is what dads are supposed to do. One thing about my dad is that he tapes all of the games that I am in. So he ends up doing his own scouting on me."

His father's scouting rarely happens in person. "My dad's been at a few of my games, but honestly," Farnsworth disclosed, "he'd rather watch it on the television. Probably this way, he can always be there to tape it."

He may not often be there in person, but Farnsworth still knows that his dad is very proud of his son. "He is my biggest fan!" added Farnsworth with a big smile.

◆ CHONE FIGGINS ◆

Desmond DeChone Figgins grew up in Florida and has played in the majors since 2002 for the Angels and Mariners. But as a kid, the future major-league All-Star didn't even believe he was the best baseball player in his family.

"My dad was my coach mostly through Little League. I had a brother that was three years older than me and a lot better player," said Figgins, who goes by the name, Chone (pronounced SHAWN). "My dad, on the other hand, never accepted that and because I was his son and on his team, he wasn't going to take it easy on me. I was expected to hold my own. My dad never wanted to play favorites or show favoritism. He didn't want me to get off easy. He really stressed that growing up."

Figgins recognized what his father was trying to accomplish by pushing him. "A lot of times, if he saw us slacking off, he'd remind me I wasn't being a good teammate. It wasn't that he was trying to be hard on me; his goal was to make me better. My dad wanted me to respect the game and respect the fact that I was given tremendous God-given talents—to play this type of sport and appreciate what you are playing because of these God-given talents. Some kids don't have the opportunity to play. You do have the opportunity to play and you have to appreciate and be thankful for that."

Figgins graduated from Brandon High School, where he was voted team MVP as a junior and third-team High School All-American as a senior in 1997. He was selected that year in the 4th round of the June draft by the Colorado Rockies. He was traded to the Anaheim Angels on July 13, 2001, and made his major-league debut shortly thereafter, on August 25, 2002.

"It was in Boston and my parents came to see me play at Fenway," said the infielder/outfielder. "To have that as my first opportunity in the big leagues and for it to be in Boston made it doubly nervous for me. The fans that day were great for me. I even ended up scoring a run to win the game and they congratulated me. But that is why Boston fans are so unique ... they appreciate the game."

But they aren't his biggest fans. "My parents and brother are my biggest fans," stated Figgins. "My brother is probably my biggest fan because he pretty much got me to this point as a player. So I think he is the most appreciative of them all."

◆ JEFF FRANCOEUR ◆

Almost every little boy who plays baseball dreams of making it to the big leagues one day and playing for his childhood team. It doesn't happen often, but every once in awhile that dream comes true. It did for Jeff Francoeur.

"I grew up in the Atlanta area and being a Braves fan," stated the Brave's first selection in the June 2002 draft. "I started T-ball in 1991 when the Braves won their first division title, so growing up I like to say I've only known a winner," he added with a smile.

"I pinch myself every day I'm here," he continued. "It really is a boyhood dream that came true for me. Playing baseball is what I wanted to do ever since I was little and I get to play it every day and that's what makes it so much fun."

When Francoeur was growing up in the Atlanta area, surrounded by a family of teachers, his father, David, was always his coach, at least in baseball. "He loved football and basketball, but he never coached me in either of those two sports. He was always more of a baseball kind of guy. I can never remember my dad sitting in the stands. He was always the coach. That was great for me and a thrill for me."

His dad was not his coach in the big leagues, but he was in attendance for his son's major-league debut on July 7, 2005, when Francoeur started in right field in the second game of a doubleheader against the Cubs. "It's funny," the younger Francoeur recalled, "in my entire career and whatever sport I played—football, basketball or baseball, or whatever—I never knew my dad to cheer. He would always clap after I did something. He is a humble guy. But after I hit my first big-league home run, in my first game, I saw him on tape in the stands going crazy. I never saw my dad so excited. At that very moment, I knew my dad was very proud."

A proud moment for dad, but his son pays tribute to him every day. "My dad taught me to be a 'never quit' kind of guy," Francoeur stated. "He never pushed me into the sport. But he told me if I were to play, then be the best at it. In fact, he never let me settle for mediocrity. The way I play is a reflection upon him."

"I have always loved this game," Francoeur continued. "The game has always been a thrill and a pleasure to play, but it is not what defines me as a person, nor is it the only thing that makes me happy. Each day I try to keep this in mind. My dad always taught me to be polite." And polite is actually what Francoeur is all about. With his perpetual kidlike smile Francoeur is always there to share a moment or an autograph with a fan. "My dad always taught me to give another person the respect you would want yourself. If you look at life that way, you will get through it all just fine."

Francoeur's father was not the only person to give lessons on how to treat others. One of his Braves teammates gave him some pointers, but from another perspective. "I remember when I got called up," Francoeur recounted, "John Smoltz took a bunch of the rookies out to dinner and he picked up the entire tab. When we offered to pay, he said, 'When you get to be thirty-five or thirty-six years old, just make sure you do the same for another rookie.' And that is what makes baseball so great. It's all part of the tradition that baseball is all about."

In a game like baseball, with all the ups and downs, you can never underestimate the value of having someone to turn to when you need an ear or a little advice. Francoeur still calls his father when he needs a boost, although sometimes the advice comes unsolicited.

"One year my dad flew out to Milwaukee when I was struggling a little bit. He came up there so he could help me with my swing," Francoeur reminisced fondly. "Considering he's been watching me since I was five, he knows exactly how my swing should look. Nobody knows it better. Fathers really do know best!"

The one piece of advice that his father—the teacher and coach—gave him that really stuck, according to Francoeur, is the perfect advice for any aspiring professional athlete—"Be a better guy off the field than you are on the field."

◆ SAM FULD ◆

Sam Fuld is a rarity in Major League Baseball. He is one of only a handful of Jewish players currently in the major leagues; he is one of very few players to turn down an opportunity to start his professional career after being drafted in his junior year of college because he wanted to complete his degree; he is an outfielder under five feet ten inches and he plays baseball at the highest level despite having to continually regulate his type 1 diabetes.

But Fuld doesn't look at himself any differently than he does any other player. He credits his father with investing him with perseverance and emotional balance. "My first year of playing Little League he was my coach," said Fuld. "I must have been five years old and he started coaching me. He pretty much coached me all the way through Little League. He also helped out with my American Legion teams. So, basically, he was my coach all the way through high school at various levels."

Fuld said that his father Ken, the dean of the College of Liberal Arts at the University of New Hampshire, taught him well. "I think he did a pretty good job of preaching to me the benefits of the work ethic and discipline, but he also had this way of balancing that with me having fun," said Fuld. "First and foremost he wanted me to have fun. We played countless hours with him throwing me batting practice and hitting me fly balls. He also recognized when it started to get frustrating for me out there. My dad would say, 'Okay that's enough.' He was good at understanding limits. My dad was never pushy. I'd get more frustrated at myself. I'd have such high expectations for myself. I'd throw a bat every now and again, pout, and just basically act like a teenager. He had a lot of patience with me. I don't think I ever shed a tear. . . . I think I held it in pretty well."

He recalled the first obstacle he had to overcome in his baseball career. "I remember one day my dad was hitting me fly balls," said Fuld. "He was my coach and I must have been nine years old at the time. He hit this line drive shot at me into the outfield. I was camped under it and then I noticed one of my teammates walked right in front of me. I lost track of the ball and it clocked me right smack in my left eye. My teammate had blocked my vision and I'm telling you my eye and that side of my face looked like a grapefruit. So my dad rushed me to the hospital. I think he was particularly worried because he had studied vision research for his teaching. All the way to the hospital he was thinking about all the potential hazards of an eye injury. It was a scary moment for both him and me, but fortunately I survived."

When Fuld was ten years old, he was diagnosed with type 1 diabetes. Soon after, the New Hampshire native tried to find major leaguers who also had type 1 diabetes. He found more than a few. Through Rich Gale, a friend of the family who was the Red Sox pitching coach at the time, Fuld met pitcher Bill Gullickson before a game one night at Fenway Park. They talked for ten minutes about blood sugar levels and how best to manage those while playing ball. "It was a brief conversation, but it did mean a lot to me," Fuld said. "To meet a Major League Baseball player who had type 1 diabetes like me was huge."

Fuld said he wants to share his story with any young athlete dealing with needles and glucometers. "My goal is to never let it affect me performance-wise. It's a balancing act, and it can be done."

Fuld graduated from Phillips Exeter Academy, a prep school in New Hampshire. He then went to Stanford University, where he became the school's and the Pac 10's all-time leader in runs scored (268) before graduating in 2004 with a degree in economics. He had been selected by the Chicago Cubs in the 24th round of the June draft in 2003, but did not sign. They selected him again in 2004, this time in the 10th round.

He signed with the Cubs to take the next step to achieving his lifelong dream of being a Major League Baseball player, then yet another obstacle emerged. In his second-to-last game at Stanford, he broke his shoulder, tore his labrum, and partially tore his rotator cuff diving for a ball, requiring a year of rehabilitation.

Fuld finally began his professional career in 2005 and made it to the majors on September 5, 2007. He has made a name for himself with his acrobatic defense, becoming a human highlight reel who gives little thought to sparing his body. Fans of the Tampa Bay Rays, who acquired Fuld in a 2011 trade with the Cubs, certainly appreciate his gusty play and have nicknamed Fuld "Super Sam" for those same acrobatic and courageous efforts.

◆ J. J. FURMANIAK ◆

"My father was a big part of my life growing up. Most important, it was his insights into life and the support system he provided. I even had a brother who was four years older than me that he coached, too. But my dad was always at every game even if he didn't coach me at that particular point in my Little League career," revealed major-league infielder J. J. Furmaniak.

"I remember they had this T-ball parade," said Furmaniak. "I remember everyone's name was on this banner. I remember seeing my name and being there with my dad holding the banner. It was cool and I'll never forget that experience as long as I live."

Furmaniak said he learned lessons from his father that stayed with him long after his Little League days were done. "My dad worked really hard. At times he had two jobs as I grew up," recalled the Illinois native. "I guess I remember the work ethic he always had and how I have that today. It was a great lesson he taught me. It was the determination he had to support our family. I remember he was constantly getting up early and working late and it was that work ethic that has paid off for me in the long run."

Furmaniak graduated from Bolingbrook High School and went on to Lewis University. In 2002, he was selected by the San Diego Padres in the 22nd round of the June draft. On July 28, 2005, he was traded to the Pittsburgh Pirates and was finally given the opportunity he had been waiting for.

Just forty-seven days after the trade, on September 13, the Pirates called him up and he started the game at second base. "It was really cool!" Furmaniak excitedly recalled. "I was with the Pirates and I got called up during a series in St. Louis in 2005. Growing up just outside of Chicago playing a game in St. Louis meant that my family was only a four to five hour drive away. My whole family was there and it was a great experience. And, when you are playing in St. Louis there is generally 35,000 red shirts in the stadium so my family of ten had the only black shirts on. Even though they were the only black shirts out there, the St. Louis Cardinals fans near them—knowing why they were there—were very supportive. They even stood up with my family and clapped when I got my first major-league hit," reminisced Furmaniak of the double in the seventh inning he hit off Chris Carpenter.

Furmaniak has bounced between the majors and minors for much of his career, but he still has the great work ethic that his father instilled in him. "Now that I've been playing at this higher level, my father doesn't always give a lot of advice," revealed Furmaniak. "My father is very smart about that. But when I was in the minors he was always there. He was always good at saying and reminding me about the things that got me here. He would always say things like, 'Remember when you used to do this or that when you were younger.' That is what I mean by the positive support system he provided."

◆ JAIME GARCIA ◆

"My earliest memory was going with my dad every Sunday and watching him play ball. I must have been just three years old and I remember playing with all the other kids there. But even back then, I knew baseball was going to be my sport," reminisced Jaime Garcia, a left-handed pitcher for the St. Louis Cardinals.

Garcia grew up in Mexico, where his father coached him throughout Little League. "My dad didn't play a lot of baseball, he played here and there," shared Garcia. "We kind of learned together."

Garcia said the most important thing he learned from his dad was about hard work. "My father is a man that has done a lot of things on his own and is very responsible. His family always meant the world to him. Everything for him had to be done 100 percent—everything from being responsible and disciplined and never take anything for granted. And don't think about giving 50 percent or 70 percent. He always gave 100 percent to everything he did in his life," said Garcia.

"I have taken that concept and put it to work for me in my job as a major leaguer. He has always taught me, 'If you go to school or play baseball, whatever you do or career you choose, you must give 100 percent to that effort.' That is what he has done in his life and I have watched him, and I have learned from him."

The six foot two starter went to Sharyland High School in Mission, Texas. He was selected by the Baltimore Orioles in the 30th round of the June 2004 draft, but a mandatory test given to all draftees was interpreted incorrectly and held up his signing. As a result, Garcia returned to Sharyland. But he found he was too old to play for the high school baseball team in 2005. Fortunately, the scout who originally scouted Garcia moved on to the Cardinals and convinced them to select him in the 22nd round of the 2005 draft.

Garcia went on to make his major-league debut in relief on July 11, 2008, in Pittsburgh. His career then took a detour, as he missed the entire 2009 season recovering from Tommy John surgery. Thanks to his 100 percent effort at rehabilitating his surgically repaired arm, Garcia made an amazing comeback in 2010 and has been a staple in the Cardinals starting rotation ever since.

His father remains an important part of his life. "I still talk to him all the time," said Garcia. "He will always be my father and I will always be his son. I love my father and he will always be my biggest fan and he will always be there to support me."

◆ NICK GREEN ◆

Sometimes, it's not the number of years a father spends as his son's coach, but the quality of the time he spends with his son every day that's most important. That was the case for Nick Green.

Green's father was his coach for just one year, when he was thirteen. But Green has greater memories—and a greater appreciation—of his father's daily involvement in his and his twin brother Kevin's lives as their unofficial coach and teacher. "I appreciate the fact how each day he'd come home from work, change his clothes, and he'd take me and my brother to the park to hit," said Green. "The older I get, the more I appreciate what he did and him being my dad."

The versatile infielder continued: "My dad was always there to pick me and my brother up even when things were going bad. He never forced anything on us. My dad was there to support us in whatever we did."

Green went on to Georgia Perimeter Junior College after graduating from Duluth High School and was selected by the Atlanta Braves in the 32nd round of the June 1998 draft. After over five years in the minors, he finally made his major-league debut on May 15, 2004, against the Milwaukee Brewers and got his first major-league hit in his third at-bat.

Unfortunately, Green's father was not able to attend his major-league debut, but he was able to catch him in a game against the Arizona Diamondbacks just three days later. The game was memorable for both father and son on many levels. "The first game he attended was Randy Johnson's perfect game, when I played for the Braves," Green explained. "It was definitely one to remember. Yet, even though it was a perfect game, nothing could compare to him seeing his son play in a big-league game. It didn't matter to him what was going on in the field."

Needless to say, Green's parents are proud of him. "My dad and mom have always wanted me and my brother to be happy and do what we want to do," said Green. "For me, playing in the big leagues is a dream come true."

Like many other major leaguers, Green still speaks to his father often. "We talk all the time and it's not so much how to hit or how to throw or about baseball technique anymore. It's just to talk, father and son."

◆ SHAWN GREEN ◆

"My dad was my coach in Little League, Pony League, and then up to high school," said two-time MLB All-Star Shawn Green. "I can still remember myself playing T-ball. I was on the Twins!"

The six foot four outfielder/first baseman learned a lot from his father and was philosophical when trying to think of the greatest lesson he learned from him. "You learn so much from your father," said Green. "But if I was to say one thing, it would probably be the concept of hard work and the work ethic."

Green graduated from Tustin High School in 1991, the same year he was selected by the Toronto Blue Jays in the first round (16th overall) of the June draft. He made his major-league debut at the tender age of twenty, on September 28, 1993, at Milwaukee. He played with the Blue Jays from 1993 to 1999, before being traded and playing for the Los Angeles Dodgers from 2000 to 2004. Green finished his career by playing just under two years in Arizona and just over one year with the New York Mets.

"I played five years for Los Angeles, where I'm from, so it was like playing in my own backyard. My parents, therefore, got to attend a lot of games while I played for Los Angeles. Being an hour away from Dodger Stadium helped them be there for me," said Green.

"It was a dream. I always wanted to be a big leaguer," Green mused. "I am so fortunate that I have been able to fulfill my dream. I also know it is a lot of kids' dream out there. I was very fortunate to play and compete at that level."

◆ TOBY HALL ◆

Major League Baseball catcher Toby Hall hit a very memorable inside-the-park home run. "Well, it was in Little League, during T-ball," admitted Hall. "It was the only time I ever got an inside-the-park home run. Then again, there was no fence, so I just kept running!"

The California native had a lot of baseball guidance growing up with his father and older brother. "My dad was mine and my brother's coach back in Little League," said Hall. "I must have been five years old. He continued being my coach up until I was twelve years old. My brother, Todd, went on to play for the White Sox and it was nice having that guidance growing up, too."

Todd was drafted by the Chicago White Sox in 1993, but only lasted one season in their organization. Toby was selected by the Tampa Bay Devil Rays in the 9th round of the June 1997 draft and climbed through the minors until making his major-league debut on September 15, 2000.

He soon found out that getting to the major leagues is only half the battle; the other half is staying there. Hall, who has played for the Devil Rays, Dodgers, and White Sox said the key to success is having your family's support. "My dad is always there to give encouragement," said the six foot three catcher. "He would say, 'Hey, don't let it get you down and don't get frustrated. Just go back to the basics.' It's good to hear those words every once in awhile because in this business you normally hear it coming from all different levels. But when you hear it from your pop it is good to hear."

Hall continued, "Dads really do seem to have this intuition of what we go through out there. They are the ones who have seen us play since we were little."

◆ ROY HALLADAY ◆

"My dad was my coach early on, beginning in T-ball and then in coach-pitch," said six foot six Harry Leroy Halladay III (a.k.a Roy Halladay or Doc Halladay). "He then moved on into an assistant coaching role throughout the rest of my Little League days. But my dad did it all, helping whenever he could."

The seven-time All-Star and two-time Cy Young winner, grew up near Denver, Colorado. The Rockies were not in existence when he was growing up. So who were his idols? "Obviously, on a personal side my idol was my dad," said Halladay. "From the baseball side, I was a big Dale Murphy fan growing up. I liked watching him; he always seemed like a good person and a solid player. They were my two biggest idols growing up."

After graduating from Arvada West High School in 1995, the ultra-competitive Halladay was selected by the Toronto Blue Jays in the first round (17th overall) of the June draft. He rose quickly through the minors and made his major-league debut on September 20, 1998, at Tampa Bay.

"The first time I pitched in the big leagues, I had my dad there," Halladay recalled. "He made the special trip just to see me. It was kind of fun to have him there and it was special for me."

Halladay went on to pitch over ten seasons with the Blue Jays, before signing with the Philadelphia Phillies in 2010. On May 29, 2010, against the Florida Marlins, Halladay became only the twentieth pitcher in Major League Baseball history to throw a perfect game. He went on to throw a no-hitter in the first game of the National League Division Series against the Cincinnati Reds on October 6, 2010, recording just the second post-season no-hitter in MLB history. Combined with his perfect game against the Marlins in May, the playoff no-hitter vs. the Reds made Halladay just the fifth player in major-league history to throw two no-hitters in the same calendar year.

His father, a commercial pilot, "follows my career closely and keeps in touch when he can," said a thoughtful Halladay. "Today, he is more supportive than baseball wise. But he is always there for me."

◆ JACK HANNAHAN ◆

"My dad was my coach during my Little League days," said Minnesota native Jack Hannahan. "Growing up he was always there for me. We used to live right across the street from a public school, so me and my older brother, Buzz, would be playing ball on their fields all the time. My brother even got the opportunity to play for the Phillies organization for nine years. And, our dad was always there hitting ground balls and throwing batting practice to us."

Hannahan's father, John, produced two professional baseball players, so what was the greatest lesson he taught?

"Tough to say," said Hannahan. "There were so many lessons he taught us. I always remember him saying to respect the game and always play it like it should be played. I remember my dad pulled me off the field during one of my high school games. He was in the stands and he yelled at me to come in and tuck in my shirt and to pull my pants up higher because it was part of the game. He would always stress to us to hustle and said, 'There's always someone watching.'"

In 1998, Hannahan graduated from Cretin-Durham High School, the same school that produced Minnesota greats Joe Mauer and Paul Molitor. He went on to the University of Minnesota where he was named Big 10 Player of the Year and First-Team All-Big 10 in his 2001 junior year. That same year, he was selected by the Detroit Tigers in the 3rd round of the June draft.

The major-league infielder made his debut on May 25, 2006, five years after starting his professional career. "I still talk to my dad every day," admitted Hannahan, "and he's always got something to say! In the minor leagues I would always get a call from him in the morning and he would always tell me who was pitching against us that night and then would go on and give advice on how to face him. Like, 'Hey, this guy has a lot of walks so be patient at the plate.' My brother and I would call him the 'Stat Rat.'"

Hannahan said his father has done a lot more than help him become a better baseball player. "My dad was the one who helped turn me into a man," he insisted. "There was always some great lesson he taught me, some I would figure out right away and some I still had to learn the hard way. But my dad has been with me through thick and thin and he continues to stand by me and will always be my biggest supporter."

◆ JEREMY HERMIDA ◆

Only one person in Major League Baseball history has hit a pinch-hit home run in his first MLB at-bat, and that person is Jeremy Hermida.

His road to the majors was much like many others. It began in Marietta, Georgia, with Little League. "My dad was always a part of the coaching staff when I played—beginning at age six, and then all the way up to when I was thirteen years old," said Hermida.

"He was around after that every day doing what dads would do on the field," Hermida continued. "And I know he's still there, watching the games for me and looking at game tapes and relaying advice back to me."

The outfielder went on to Wheeler High School and took a key piece of advice from his father with him. "My father taught me that you are only as good as your next at-bat. It was something he always preached to me," explained Hermida. "When I was growing up, it could be easy to get comfortable. One at-bat you might be the hero and hit the home run that will win the game and the next at-bat you might strike out. This game kind of humbles you, and that is what keeps it level for me even today."

As a senior in 2002, Hermida became a first-round selection (11th overall) in the draft for the Florida Marlins, and was named the Best Pure High School Hitter in the draft by *Baseball America*.

"I was always with him every chance I could," Hermida said of his father. "I remember my father telling me how much his own dad loved being with him and that is why I think he loved sharing time with me. He was always there having fun with me and teaching me.

"What I remember the most," he continued, "was the times when he would just hit me balls and have a catch with me whenever he could."

Hermida got the call to the majors on August 31, 2005, and hit a grand slam off Al Reyes and the St. Louis Cardinals, but his father missed the big moment. "My dad was actually there for my second game," he said of the September 3 contest vs. the New York Mets. "In this business you don't always know when you are going to be called up to the big leagues. But he was there."

Hermida doesn't have to seek out his father for advice. "My dad's funny. He gets bored at home at times and I often find him looking at old games and comparing them with some current games to see if I am looking the same or if I'm struggling," he explained. "My dad has and always will be there for me."

♦ AARON HILL ♦

Aaron Hill grew up in Visalia, California. Like many boys, he loved to play baseball. "It was in Little League," he said of his first baseball memory. "It wasn't a big game, but it was the first game I helped win when the game was in the final innings. I remember hitting a line drive over the second baseman's head and it won the game. I remember my dad picking me up after the game and holding me. Little League still holds some of those neat memories I had as a kid."

The infielder had his father as his coach for most of his youth. "Pretty much whenever my dad could be involved, he was there," said Hill. "My dad was really involved in coaching and it just so happened that both of his boys played sports, so he got to coach us in baseball and soccer. He was my coach up to junior high."

The greatest lesson Hill said he learned from his coach-father was a baseball basic. "I used to get in trouble if I didn't run a ball out to first base," Hill recalled. "He used to get upset with me if I didn't run a ball out. I remember he used to carry around this cartoon of a pelican, which had this frog halfway in his mouth, and his hands were up to his throat as though he was choking and the caption on the cartoon read, 'Never give up.' I will always remember that cartoon and its meaning."

After graduating from Redwood High School, Hill was selected by the Anaheim Angels in the 7th round of the June 2000 draft. He did not sign, but instead went on to Louisiana State University. He was selected again three years later, this time by the Toronto Blue Jays in the first round (13th overall).

Hill made his major-league debut with the Blue Jays less than two years later, on May 20, 2005, with his dad in attendance. "You can never forget that," he stated. "And, I will never forget the grin my dad had on his face that went from ear to ear. It was fun for us all. It was definitely a good memory."

Hill's father is not his coach anymore, but it's tough to take the coach out of the father. "Sometimes I turn to him for advice," Hill grinned, "but today he'll say things like, 'Just relax and have fun!' He'll also say things like, 'You know how to pre-pare. You know what to do, so go out there and play.'"

◆ ERIC HINSKE ◆

Eric Hinske's father was a teacher and doubled as his coach throughout most of his life. "My dad was my coach all through Little League and then all the way up through high school. He was my coach in Little League, Pony League, Babe Ruth League, and everything else," said the easygoing Hinske with a grin.

However, sometimes having your father as a coach is not easy, according to Hinske. "Because I was his son, he was a little harder on me," Hinkse explained. "I remember being mad at him quite a bit in high school because he was my coach and was always yelling at me. But then I'd come home and my mom used to tell me that 'he really does love you and he really does mean well.' At the time, you weren't always thinking that was the case, but I don't get mad at him anymore."

Hinske played a lot of baseball because he loved the game and claims that "pretty much from day one, I knew I wanted to be a ballplayer." It's a dream many kids have when growing up, but when Hinske received a scholarship to play for the University of Arkansas, he "decided to really give a big-league career a go."

He went off to college without the coach who had guided him through his entire life, but he did take at least one important lesson with him. "My dad always kept it simple," Hinske explained. "He'd always say, 'Play the game the right way and approach it that way.'"

His diligence at college paid off when the Chicago Cubs selected him in the 17th round of the June 1998 draft. Hinske was subsequently traded to the Oakland Athletics in March 2001, then again to the Toronto Blue Jays in December 2001.

The Wisconsin native made his major-league debut on April 1, 2002, at third base. "My dad was there for my first game in 2002," said Hinske. "It was Opening Day at Fenway Park and I was playing the Red Sox. My whole family came out to see me and it was pretty cool."

Hinske went on to earn American League Rookie of the Year honors in 2002 and appear in three straight World Series with three different teams, winning a world title in 2007 with the Red Sox and another with the Yankees in 2009 but falling just short with the Rays in 2008. His father still follows—and brags about—his star player. "He likes to talk," laughed the outfielder. "He comes to games all of the time. He is retired now, but even when he worked he was a teacher, so he had the summers off."

Now a father of two, Hinske still turns to his father for advice. "Not as much about baseball anymore, because I'm on a different level of play now," he explained. "I remember talking to him in the past when I struggled or when things were going bad, but that was more for his fatherly advice and influence. It is the confidence thing he helps me the most about these days. He helps me to realize what is going on and then helps me turn it around."

◆ TREVOR HOFFMAN ◆

Trevor Hoffman is the model of what a professional baseball player should be like, not only on the field, but also off it. And his father, Ed, the singing usher, deserves the credit for instilling those values in him.

"My dad loved us unconditionally more than anything," said Hoffman, himself a father of three sons. "It wasn't a lesson necessarily, but rather it has been a great lesson I've been able to pass on to my kids. My father was always very patient and was always there for us."

Hoffman's father was an ex-Marine and a professional singer who gave up his career to be with his family. It was then that he started working at the post office and, for fun, became an usher at Anaheim Stadium. He also took the time to coach Little League.

"The thing I remember about Little League was that it was all about getting that dollar after the game so you could go to the snack bar afterward for some candy or a hot dog or something," Hoffman recalled with a smile.

"Another thing I remember, and this was pretty cool, my dad would always sing the national anthem for Opening Day ceremonies in Little League. My dad was an entertainer. He ultimately got the chance to sing the national anthem for some games at Anaheim Stadium when they needed someone (and did so several times). I remember he even sang the national anthem the night Roger Clemens broke into the game with the Red Sox in 1981. I thought that was pretty cool. I remember right before he died, he got to sing the national anthem one final time and it made me cry," said Hoffman, thinking back to 1995.

When he retired, the all-time career saves leader (601) in Major League Baseball history, Hoffman has two brothers who are more than a decade older than him. His oldest brother, Greg, coached high school basketball for many years and his other brother, Glen, played almost a decade in the majors as an infielder, and remains in the game as a coach.

"I remember my dad loved watching us play all the time when we were little," recalled the seven-time All-Star. "He'd say he watched better games in the backyard than on any big league field. It didn't matter—Wiffle ball, or basketball, whatever we played he enjoyed watching us and he enjoyed having his family around him. . . . He lived a happy life."

An eighteen-year major leaguer, Trevor Hoffman played his last MLB game on September 29, 2010, and is sure to be elected to the Hall of Fame. "It all goes back to my family," said the humble Hoffman. "The Wiffle-ball games in the backyard. The influence of my two brothers, who taught me so much. Learning humility from my parents, how they made people around them feel good about themselves. And all the baseball people along the way that came into my life at just the right time."

◆ MATT HOLLIDAY ◆

Baseball is a family business in the Holliday house. "My dad grew up in the Pittsburgh area and later spent some time in the minor-league organization for the Pirates," said Matt Holliday, a major-league outfielder. "He spent a few years there and then he got involved with coaching at the college level. My dad spent twenty-five years coaching for Oklahoma State and seven of those years as their head coach. My dad then moved on to the University of Texas as their pitching coach. He's been a coach for a long time and in between all of that time, he coached me.

"It's been a family affair for me in baseball. My dad has been a driving force in my own career. Once again, baseball has always been a part of our family."

Holliday's father, Tom, is currently the head coach at North Carolina State and his brother, Josh, is assistant baseball coach at Vanderbilt University. Wanting to stay in the "family business," Matt Holliday established himself as a major leaguer and perennial All Star.

"My dad never pushed me toward baseball, he always wanted me to do whatever I wanted to do and to be happy," said Holliday. "But I have always wanted to be a baseball player . . . ever since I was a little kid. Growing up around the game, I've always loved baseball, and being around it as a kid really helped.

"I remember when I was younger we'd travel a lot of times during the summer to the West Coast," Holliday continued. "As a family we'd go and see all of the major-league stadiums. We'd go out and see the Giants and Dodgers game and then we would go and see all the games in the series. It was our summer vacation and it was fun!"

The Colorado Rockies' 7th-round selection in the June 1998 draft doesn't get as much direction from his father anymore, but "every day he is there for me for advice. It's not so much as it used to be. I'm at a higher level now and I know my swing pretty good now, but he is still there to give me encouragement and advice," he said.

"Probably the greatest lesson I learned from my dad was the concept of hard work," he said. "I used to admire all the hard work he put into his job and how dedicated he was in helping to turn the program at Oklahoma State around."

◆ PHIL HUGHES ◆

Phil Hughes grew up in Mission Viejo, California, just outside of Anaheim Stadium, yet he was a Red Sox fan as a kid. That can be attributed to his father, who grew up just outside of Fenway Park in Boston. The entire family changed allegiances however when the New York Yankees selected young Phil in the first round (23rd overall) of the June 2004 draft out of high school.

Thinking back, Hughes credits his father with much of his success. "My dad started coaching me at age ten and continued right up before high school. It seems when your dad is your coach he has a tendency to get onto you more than the other kids. He was never afraid of telling me what he thought—especially when he didn't think I was playing up to my potential. For the other kids, he let them slide a little more. Eventually, that helped me to learn discipline. My dad spent fifteen years in the Navy and he was one that definitely knew discipline. I don't regret that he was my coach. It was great that he was because I wouldn't have learned the game as well as I did without him."

The six foot five right-hander went to Foothill High School, where he set the school record for most career wins (23). He went 12–0 in his junior year and 9–1 in his senior year, when he also notched a perfect game. But his perfect game and wins are not what he remembers most about those days.

"Every day I would play baseball," Hughes recalled. "I remember I was on the high school team and practices would sometimes cut into my school day. And that was the kind of thing that made being a kid fun. School was a big part of growing up, but being on the field all day and then going home just when it started to get dark are the memories I will always keep."

Hughes recalled keeping up his childhood baseball routine, even on his birthday. "I also remember having to go to practice on my birthday all the time. My birthday falls in June, during summer ball," said Hughes of his June 24 birthday. "I never wanted to go to practice on that day, but my dad always insisted I go. He'd always say 'We'll have your birthday tomorrow.' So all through my kid years, my birthday was celebrated on June 25, it was like Lincoln's birthday, like it was some sort of special observance day."

Hughes made his major-league debut on April 26, 2007, against the Toronto Blue Jays at Yankee Stadium. He has gone on to earn a World Series Championship ring in 2009 and be named to the American League All-Star team in 2010. But he's gone through some tough times, too, including several trips to the disabled list.

"Any time I find myself struggling with something," Hughes shared, "I know my dad's been through it all before. Even when I don't call, he'll leave these hour-long voice mails on my phone about everything I need to remember. He especially leaves a message on my phone if he watches the game and knows I struggled a little bit. He'll leave questions on my answering machine like, 'Was your sinker working?' Then I call him back and say, 'I don't throw a sinker.' Then he'll call back up and say, 'Then why don't you throw one next time, or learn one?'"

But it's not just about baseball. "I still call my dad a lot when I need something," said Hughes. "For example, I get this stuff all the time in the mail. I have no idea what it is and then it's time to call my dad. He's good at all of that kind of stuff. I'll say to him, 'I don't know what I just got in the mail,' and then I'll send it to him and he generally fills it out and then all I'll have to do is sign it. It's funny, you think things would change when you move out and you're on your own, but he's still always going to be your dad."

◆ BRANDON INGE ◆

Brandon Inge's father coached him and his brother from the ages of five through twelve. According to the major leaguer, his father had some baseball experience in college and shared that experience with his sons.

His ability to coach his sons was cut short by a freak accident, but the younger Inge shared the story to show the depth of his father's character. "When I was fourteen or fifteen years old," Inge began, "my father was on a business trip and the hotel he was staying at had a power failure. Prior to the power failure he had pulled a table over so he could eat his dinner and still watch the television. When the power went out, he got up and accidentally walked right into a wrought-iron chandelier and it jabbed him in the eye.

"When they took him to the hospital to sew it up, it still left him blind in one eye. And for a guy who used to throw me and my brother batting practice, who used to have catches with us and used to help us with our baseball all of the time, it absolutely crushed him. It was devastating, because when you don't have two good eyes, you have a problem when it comes to depth of field. The loss of the eye made it extremely difficult to catch a ball. So after he had his eye removed and a glass one was put in, he would go outside and start throwing a tennis ball up in the air and attempt to catch it as a way of figuring out his depth perception. He did all this because he wanted to get back to throwing batting practice to me and my brother. That was his main concern and inspiration for doing what he did. My dad didn't care about himself, or how much it hurt, he just worried he wasn't going to be able to play catch with his sons anymore.

"He eventually came back from it and was able to pitch and have a catch with us again," Inge continued. "I remember my brother and I used to try and make him feel better by holding our hand over one eye and having a catch. It's not that easy. My dad had this ability to make a bad situation into a positive. He always reminded us that it doesn't matter what happens, you can still work hard and make it through anything."

It was a good thing his father was involved with him and his early baseball career, as he held the key to Inge's future success.

"The best thing he taught me, baseball-wise, was his ability to help focus my temper," Inge confessed. "When I was growing up I used to have a little temper, which I don't have any more. My dad taught me not to disrespect the game of baseball by throwing helmets or throwing bats or throwing temper tantrums. He told me that it was all right to be mad and it's fine to feel that way, but to keep it to yourself and use it in a positive way when you get out to the field. He would say, 'Put that anger into your play.' He would also say to me that throwing helmets and throwing bats isn't helpful to your team either. It looks bad in front of your teammates. Treat them with respect . . . and that is something I have always remembered.

"Look, everyone is going to have a moment," Inge added, "even in the big leagues, and actually even more so at times in the big leagues because you're always under the microscope, but the thing is, I've been able to bottle it up and use it more productively instead of trashing a dugout. I've used it for the good and that is the most important lesson I've learned from my dad about baseball."

The greatest lesson he learned from his father in his personal life, however, was the Golden Rule. "My dad always stressed, treat someone as you want to be treated yourself."

So who better to serve as his boyhood idol than the epitome of a class athlete—Cal Ripken Jr. Inge, an eleven-year major leaguer, still remembers feeling as giddy as a kid when he met his childhood idol. "I admired Cal Ripken Jr. for a lot of different reasons. For me he was a great athlete. He was one of the better third basemen and shortstops of the game. Secondly, Ripken was a class act through and through. He was someone you'd like to model your kids after. I would tell my kids to sit down and watch this guy and how he plays the game and how he interacts with the fans. For me, he was the quintessential ballplayer, even today. I have an autographed picture I got from him when I was in my rookie year. It is very special to me and I have it hanging in my game room. It's funny: I never get starstruck around this game. For instance, I never get concerned as to who you are; I just want to beat you in the field. That is why I don't have that starstruck attitude. But when it comes to Ripken, that is a different story. He was the one player that made me feel like I am a kid again. He is the one guy in all of baseball, because of his humility, who made you feel good about the game."

Inge was selected by the Detroit Tigers in the 2nd round of the June 1998 draft. Initially signed as a catcher, he has caught and played center field in the majors, but his main position has become third base.

His father made it to his major-league debut on April 3, 2001. "Ironically, I wasn't supposed to be in the big leagues, but in spring training the catcher who was going to be on the roster got injured and I got catapulted right into the catching position," Inge recalled. "I remember it was Opening Day in Detroit and it was a packed house with sixty thousand fans, and my dad was there.

He added, "He's big on taking pictures, so I must have a million pictures of that first day."

"My dad's proud [of me]," Inge noted, "but he doesn't go around bragging a lot about his son being in the major leagues. He's humble, but very proud. All I know is that if my son was in a similar situation, I'd be bubbling!"

Brandon Inge is the father of two sons, Chase and Tyler, whose names are featured on a large tattoo on each of his forearms (Tyler on the right and Chase on the left). All the wisdom his father imparted with him is being shared with his own sons and if he's lucky they will be as grateful to him as he is to his dad.

Inge said he still talks to his dad all the time, "It's not so much how to hit or how to throw or about baseball technique anymore. It's just to talk, father and son."

◆ CONOR JACKSON ◆

Not every father-and-son experience is Hallmark card material. Just ask Conor Jackson. "My dad was my coach when I turned five up until I was seven years old," Jackson began. "When I got a little older he was still coaching, but we were on different teams because we didn't always get along. We were like oil and water at times. He expected a lot out of me and it was the best situation for the two of us."

Jackson's father was more of a football and basketball guy, but he still did what he could in baseball. "My dad was always the guy who threw me batting practice every day," Jackson explained. "He was always there for me. Over the years we kind of learned the game together."

The six foot two MLB outfielder shared another recollection from his early baseball days. "My first memory growing up playing baseball was my first coach-pitch home run. It was also the only one hit in the league that season," said Conor. "I still have a picture of it as I was running home and was surrounded by my teammates. It was a pretty big moment for me."

After graduating from El Camino Real High School in 2000, Conor went to the University of California, Berkley, where he actually played third base. Following his junior year, he was selected by the Arizona Diamondbacks in the first round (19th overall) of the June 2003 draft.

A short two years later, he made his major-league debut at Wrigley Field on July 28, 2005. It proved to be . . . a bittersweet moment. "My dad was working when I first got called up in 2005," said Conor of his father, an actor. "It was probably a month later that he got to see me play. It would have been nice if he was there. My first game was up in Wrigley, but he had to work and wasn't able to make it. I wish he could have been there."

◆ DESMOND JENNINGS ◆

It wasn't so long ago that Desmond Jennings was playing football and baseball with his dad as his coach. "It was fun playing for him," said the Rays' 10th round selection in the 2006 draft. "He never added any extra pressure."

Unlike many other kids, Jennings didn't have visions of playing in the majors when he got older. "I know a lot of kids say as they were growing up that being a baseball player is all they wanted to be, and that they dream about it happening, but I never thought about it. To me it was a game and I was having fun. Growing up, all sports were fun for me. It kept me going. I remember I was in high school and I wasn't that good because all I could think about was how fun it still was and that is what I still think to this day. It wasn't until my junior or senior year in high school that I even thought about going to college and playing baseball there. I knew I loved this game and it was a way for me to keep playing."

In his senior year of high school, Jennings was selected by the Cleveland Indians in the 18th round of the June 2005 draft, but he opted instead to go to college. He attended Itawamba Community College in Mississippi where he led all junior college wide receivers with 54 receptions, 8 touchdowns and 848 yards in eight football games AND hit .378 with 29 stolen bases in baseball. After one impressive season, the Tampa Bay Rays selected and signed him.

"It's funny," Jennings reflected, "I've seen a lot of dads being real tough on their kids—wanting them to do this or that—but my dad wasn't like that. Obviously he wanted me to do well, but he was always supportive. It didn't matter what sport I chose, he was going to be there and be happy for me. He did love baseball though. My dad grew up playing baseball. He loved it and it was his sport. He wanted me to play sports, but because I always wanted to please him, it made my choice easier. Because he had such a love of the game of baseball, it helped me to love the game that much more."

Jennings made his major-league debut on September 1, 2010, his father was unable to see him play on that day, but as Jennings said, "He has made up for it. Since then he has seen me play a lot. He is very proud and he loves seeing me play. He knows that this is what it is all about and why I play this game."

He still gets advice from his father. "Regardless if I ask him or not," said the outfielder, "he is always there to give it. I know he gives me advice because it's how he shows he loves me. He still sees stuff with the way I play or the way I swing the bat, and if he sees something wrong, he'll tell me. My dad will say, 'I'm just throwing it out there. . . . ' He is always there for me."

◆ DEREK JETER ◆

He may well be the contemporary face of baseball in every sense of the term. But when you see a five-time world champion and twelve-time All-Star with five Gold Gloves and four Silver Sluggers (all won while playing for the highly visible New York Yankees), you would think that surely this man had special advantages from early in life. But the biggest advantage Derek Jeter had was the support of his family.

Jeter was born in New Jersey, then moved to Kalamazoo, Michigan, when he was four years old. His father coached him in Little League for a few years. Like other kids, he had to learn tough lessons. For instance, when he wouldn't shake hands with the other team after a loss, Jeter's father told him it was "time to grab a tennis racket, since you obviously don't know how to play a team sport."

But the best lesson Jeter learned from his father was about hard work. "'You can accomplish anything you do in life if you work hard,'" Jeter recalled his father telling him. "He'd say, 'There are always going to be people better than you, but there is no reason someone should outwork you.'"

That work ethic, ingrained when he was young—as his parents would take him and his sister (a softball player) to the field to work on their skills after practice—remains with the Yankee icon to this day.

After moving to Michigan, the Jeter family would return to New Jersey to see relatives and that helped seal the young Jeter's love for the New York Yankees. He recalled when he was playing T-ball as a child, "I played on the Tigers and I always remember being a Yankees fan, so I wasn't that happy being a Tigers player and I just couldn't understand why I couldn't be a Yankee."

He did become a Yankee when the team selected him with their first pick (the 6th overall pick) in the June 1992 draft.

Three years later, he made his Major League Baseball debut on May 29 against the Mariners. "My dad was at my first game in the big leagues. He was at that game in Seattle against the Mariners and he has been there ever since," Jeter said fondly. He was even there when Jeter hit his 300th hit against David Price and the Tampa Bay Rays at Yankee Stadium in 2011.

"It has always been special to me just the fact that he has been there for me and has shown his support," Jeter concluded.

◆ CHIPPER JONES ◆

Larry Wayne Jones was a "chip" off his old man's block and thus became "Chipper." His "old man" was a very talented coach. "People tried to get my dad to coach teams that I was on ever since I was eight years old," said Jones. "He didn't ever want other kids or parents to think he was showing favoritism toward me, so I always had to prove myself on my own. My dad taught me the fundamentals of the game, but he had the other coaches take care of the discipline end of the game. It worked out great. The teaching never stopped once I left the field."

The greatest thing he learned from his dad was "patience and the work ethic," said Jones. "His big thing was, if you get the opportunity to be out there, always work to get better because there is always someone out there and they are gaining on you. There is always someone knocking on the door. That always stuck with me, especially when I was a kid. I enjoyed playing other sports—but I never enjoyed working at it as much as I enjoyed working at the game of baseball. Baseball was my passion!"

Jones graduated from the Bolles School in Jacksonville, Florida, in 1990. That same year he was selected by the Atlanta Braves as the first overall pick in the June draft. The six foot four athlete began his career as a shortstop before establishing himself as a third baseman for most of his storied career.

"I remember my dad coming down to rookie ball when I was in Bradentown, Florida. Things looked pretty grim for me back then. I wasn't playing that well and I was coming off a broken hand. I think I was batting about .220 that year and I was making a bunch of errors. It wasn't a really good first showing, especially being the Braves' first draft pick. It got me saying to myself, 'Maybe I'm not as good as I think I am.' I knew I had to work even harder."

Jones kept working and improving, and made his big-league debut on September 11, 1993, at San Diego. It was the beginning of a major-league career that so far has garnered him seven All-Star selections, a National league MVP (in 1999), two Silver Sluggers, and a world championship (in 1995).

"My dad and I still talk two or three times a week," said Jones matter-of-factly. "Whenever I get into a slump, my coaches ask me if I've called my dad. He knows my swing the best of anyone.

"We grew up in Florida, but he lives in Texas now," said Jones of his dad, who resides at the Double Dime Ranch, a working game ranch that covers 9000 high-fenced acres and is affiliated with Chipper Jones. "If it's not about the ranch I have in South Texas, then it is certainly about baseball. We always have a lot to talk about and he is really proud."

Jones is one of contemporary baseball's quintessential throwback ballplayers. He is the face of baseball in Atlanta and has a swagger that could have rivaled even the swagger of the legendary John Wayne.

"When I was younger I admired Mickey Mantle for a number of obvious reasons . . . especially, because I am a switch-hitter," revealed Jones. "When I came up I was a shortstop and I really, really looked up to three guys in particular: Barry Larkin, Ozzie Smith, and Cal Ripken Jr. I think the best glove I ever saw was Ozzie Smith. When you talk about leadership and the total package it was Larkin and Ripken." Interestingly, after his nearly two decades in the majors, Jones is considered by many in the game as the total package as well.

The key to Chipper Jones's major-league longevity? "Staying healthy," he emphatically said. "I spent the first ten years of my career without any injuries. It is always tough for me to sit on the sidelines. As time went on and injuries did occur and when I did find myself on the disabled list or not in the lineup every day, I took it as a learning opportunity. I think it actually improved my leadership qualities. I had to become more vocal because I always led silently, by example, on the field. I like to think I've blossomed into a pretty good leader over the years."

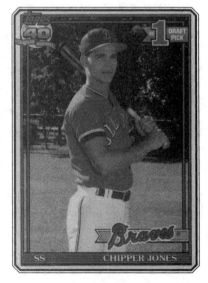

◆ MATT JOYCE ◆

Like many fathers, Matt Joyce Sr. felt so proud when his first son was born. He couldn't wait to teach him everything he knew. And in regard to baseball, he still tries to teach Matt Jr. everything he knows. "My dad was my coach all through Little League, but he still coaches nowadays," Joyce said. "My dad sends me texts every day saying things like, 'keep your head in there' or 'keep hitting it up the middle' and stuff like that. This is the way he is and has always been," a smiling Joyce said matter-of-factly.

"My dad has always helped push me and challenge me and has always helped steer me in the right direction. Basically, since I was four years old my dad has coached me officially. But in theory my dad has been my coach since I was in diapers."

The Tampa native thought back to his first baseball memory. "I remember being out in the front yard—I was very young—and my dad was pitching to me with this plastic ball and I had a plastic bat in my hands," Joyce recalled.

"I also remember when he put up a wooden board against the house where I used to hit and he used to throw to me. He'd say, 'Are you ready?' and I'd say, 'I'm ready.' Then he'd throw the ball as fast as he could by me and then say, 'I thought you said you were ready?'" laughed Joyce. "I was this little kid and I didn't have a chance. He was talking smack to me even as far back as that. My comeback would be, 'Hey, that's not fair! Come on!'"

Joyce specifically remembers one Little League All-Star game. "My dad backed up his truck behind the fence. He pulled me aside and said to me, 'If you hit the truck, you get one hundred bucks!' He added, 'I've got the hundred bucks right here waiting for you.' Sure enough, I hit a home run and hit the truck and I got the hundred bucks. So I got the money and he didn't make that bet with me again!" The outfielder went to Armwood High School in Seffner, Florida, and his devoted father attended every game he could. "When I hit high school, my dad was that dad that would yell at his kid and all of the other parents would look at him and think to themselves that he was crazy. He was tough on me and if I wasn't trying hard enough he'd be yelling at me and saying that I was swinging like a girl."

He doesn't say that Joyce swings like a girl these days. "Today he's gotten a lot more positive and has practiced positive reinforcement," Joyce laughed. "He's come a long way since then."

After high school, Joyce went on to Florida Southern University, where he helped lead his team to the Division II title in 2005. In June of that year, Joyce was selected by the Detroit Tigers in the 12th round of the draft.

Joyce made his major-league debut on May 5, 2008, against the Boston Red Sox. He was traded that winter to Tampa Bay, where he has come into his own. Joyce was named to the American League All-Star team in 2011.

His father has been by his side through it all, but Joyce had to think awhile before he could decide on the greatest lesson he learned from his dad. "I think the best lesson my dad taught me was probably to be a humble person," said Joyce, "to be thankful for everything I have, to be respectful of others, and to trust in the Lord."

◆ SCOTT KAZMIR ◆

Scott Kazmir grew up following the Houston Astros. "I liked the Killer B's—Biggio, Bagwell, and the whole gang," said Kazmir. "I particularly liked watching Billy Wagner in the closer role."

Kazmir's father did all he could for his young pitcher. "He coached me all through Little League," said Kazmir. "He did what dads do—he coached, worked the concession stand, he carpooled, but he never umpired a game. He didn't want to be the bad guy."

Sounds like the childhood enjoyed by many other young baseball players, but Kazmir's childhood led him to becoming a highly touted high school athlete. He was Cypress Falls High School's starting quarterback until his junior year, when he quit to concentrate on baseball. He threw six no-hitters during his high school career—including four consecutive no-hitters in his junior year—and was named *Baseball America*'s High School Player of the Year in 2002.

The New York Mets selected Kazmir in the first round (15th overall) of the June 2002 draft. But in a trade that still burns in the hearts and minds of Mets fans, the future All-Star was sent to the Tampa Bay Devil Rays on July 30, 2004, for Victor Zambrano.

Less than one month later, on August 23, Kazmir was in the majors, making his debut with the Devil Rays in Seattle. His parents, Eddie and Debbie, were there for his big day. "My dad actually caught a foul ball watching me pitch for the first time," said Kazmir, who chuckled when asked if he had signed the foul ball for his dad.

"It was a great experience for me," continued Kazmir. "The whole family was there for me and they got to watch me pitch."

Kazmir always knows when his dad is there. "I can always hear my dad's voice," admitted the two-time All-Star. "His voice carries and I always know where he is, no matter who is around.

"I know he is proud," continued Kazmir. "It's funny, he works with Adam Dunn's father and the two of them talk all the time."

Kazmir is now a major-league veteran, but he still reaches out to his father. "I still talk to him all the time," said the determined and sincere lefty. "We end up talking about everything," he finished with a smile.

◆ ADAM KENNEDY ◆

Most kids in high school find it embarrassing to spend a lot of time with their parents. Adam Kennedy did not have much choice. He went to J. W. North High School in California, where his father was a health teacher and coach of the baseball team. "My dad coached me my last three years in high school," recalled Kennedy.

"My dad taught me about a lot of things," said the major league second baseman. "It was good that he was my coach during those years. When you get to high school, you sometimes have a tendency to be complacent. But he was always there to make sure I wasn't falling into that trap of being complacent. Having him as my coach at that level was a great experience."

The admitted "fan of baseball" (not one certain team), went on to Cal State Northridge after high school, where he played shortstop and led the NCAA in hits his sophomore and junior seasons.

After his junior year, Kennedy became the first selection (20th overall) of the St. Louis Cardinals in the June 1997 draft. He was called up to the majors just over two years later, making his big-league debut on August 21, 1999, at Shea Stadium in New York. "My dad was there to experience it with me," recalled Kennedy. "But I was more nervous that I was playing in a stadium that had three levels to it . . . minor-league stadiums don't come with three levels. I was in the big leagues, I thought to myself!"

The 2002 American League Championship Series MVP still enjoys the big role his parents play in his life. "My mom and dad are still my biggest fans," stated Kennedy. "They are bigger fans than anybody. They have always been humble, but they are proud. My dad's a big follower of the game. He comes to a lot of games, even those on the road. He is always there and he watches my steps."

◆ IAN KINSLER ◆

Texas Rangers' second baseman Ian Kinsler spent countless hours hitting balls with his father when he was growing up in Tucson, Arizona.

"I remember going to the park every Sunday," the two-time All-Star recalled. "Everyone knew we were at the field. If anyone wanted to show up we'd be there to throw the ball around. It was better than sitting on the couch! We'd take batting practice and would hit the ball around on those days."

Kinsler's father, Howard, coached him from Little League until he was twelve. The devoted father wouldn't just throw the ball around with his son on Sundays; they spent plenty of time in the batting cages as well.

"I remember being in the batting cages for hours when I was growing up," Kinsler recalled. "My dad would be throwing to me over and over again. My dad was a switch-hitter and I remember asking him one day if he could teach me how to switch hit. He agreed and the next day we went to the batting cages and he said, 'Just remember if you are going to switch hit you have to take as many swings left-handed as you do right-handed.' I said it was fine and no big deal. Then I went ahead and hit about five to six buckets of balls and I was getting tired. Then my dad reminded me, 'Now you have to hit left-handed.' I said, 'Forget it. I don't want to switch hit anymore.' That memory sticks with me because I really had wanted to be just like him."

Kinsler went to Canyon del Oro High School where the team won state titles in 1997 and 2000. He hit .504 with 26 stolen bases in his senior year and was named to the first team All-State and first team All-League. The Arizona Diamondbacks selected him in the 29th round of the June Draft in 2000, but he felt he would benefit more from playing in college.

He attended Central Arizona College and was drafted again by the Diamondbacks, this time in the 26th round. He turned them down again, still feeling he could learn more in college. He was convinced to attend Arizona State University, but ended up spending much of the season on the bench, so he transferred to the University of Missouri for his junior year. His speed was affected by a stress fracture in his foot, but a Rangers' scout recalled his earlier speedy days and selected him in the 17th round of the June 2003 draft.

Originally a shortstop, he was switched to second base in 2005 and made his Major League debut one year later—on April 3, Opening Day, as the starting second baseman. "My dad got to see me play that day against Boston at our place in Texas in 2006. I had a lot of people there," Kinsler remembered. "I had family and friends there. It was a fun experience and I got a base hit in my first major league at-bat (off Curt Schilling). It was pretty cool."

Kinsler still stays in touch with his father, as does the advice he received from him in his youth. "Always remember where you came from and never get too high or too low. Try to stay in the middle and no matter how you are playing—good or bad—just have the same attitude always and that will equal success."

◆ STEVE KLINE ◆

"My dad was my coach all through Little League," said Steve Kline, a six foot one pitcher. "There wasn't a time he wasn't my coach!"

Thinking back on those early days, Kline recalled a story with his father. "I can remember pitching and my dad came up to me and said during a game, 'Walk this guy.' And, I said I wanted to face him. He said, 'Okay, go ahead.' The next thing I knew he hit a home run off me. So my dad said, 'See, you should have listened to your dad!'"

The lefty was born in Sunbury, Pennsylvania, and graduated from Lewisburg High School before heading to West Virginia University. He was selected by the Cleveland Indians in the 8th round of the June 1993 draft.

He made his major-league debut on April 2, 1997, in a relief appearance for the Indians at Oakland. Kline actually earned the win, getting two key outs. His career ended just over a decade later, with his final appearance on September 25, 2007.

Through it all, Kline recalled the best piece of advice his father gave him. "The greatest lesson my dad taught me growing up was to treat people like you want to be treated yourself."

◆ JOHN LACKEY ◆

"My dad was actually the assistant coach when I was in high school, but all through Little League and growing up he was my head coach," said John Lackey.

"He taught me how to compete," said the six foot six right-handed pitcher. "He stressed to me that I should know what I want and then go after it. No matter if you are doing good that day or not, you still have to go after it all the time."

Lackey grew up in Texas, so it was not surprising that he was a Texas Rangers fan and definitely a big Nolan Ryan fan. "Growing up, we'd try and go to Rangers Stadium three or so times a year and try to see Nolan Ryan at least once. That was a big thing when I was growing up," he said.

After graduating from Abilene High School in 1997, Lackey went to the University of Texas at Arlington where he played first base and tried his hand at relieving. That summer, he learned how to pitch in the Kansas Jayhawks Summer League. In 1999, he went to Grayson County Community College, where he posted a 10–3 record with a 4.23 ERA, which was good enough to catch the eye of the Anaheim Angels—the club that selected him in the 2nd round of the June draft.

He quickly ascended through the Angels minor-league system and made his major-league debut in the second game of a doubleheader against the Rangers, on June 24, 2002. "Actually, I made my debut in Texas, so it was like coming home," Lackey recalled. "I had tons of family and friends out there to see me. I had to get plenty of tickets that day. So that was something I will never forget!

"My dad was pretty excited about it," he continued. "My mom was real nervous. For me, it was a lot of fun. I felt pretty comfortable because I had been in that stadium quite a few times before watching games. Of course, I felt a little more pressure being on the field, but I just really wanted to do well because the team I was coming on to was doing pretty well and was trying to make a run for the playoffs. The whole day and game worked out well."

Lackey has had a pretty successful major-league career, and no one is more proud of him than his father. "My dad has never been the type that throws out tons of compliments and stuff like that," Lackey explained. "It's more like, 'Hey, you threw the ball pretty well last night' and that's as much as I get out of him. My dad doesn't really get into conversations with me about the technical things anymore. He knows I've got good coaches. But he is always there for support and he is the one I get to talk to about other things."

◆ MIKE LAMB ◆

Many fathers coach their sons when they are growing up . . . and some of them continue to do so throughout their sons' lives. Mike Lamb's father is one of those men.

"My dad was my coach in Pony League, when I was eleven and twelve years old," Lamb recalled. "He was also my coach for my traveling team, which went up until I was fourteen years old."

But it didn't stop there. Lamb has continued to turn to his father for advice and guidance throughout his professional career. "I turn to him primarily because he knows me better than anyone," Lamb explained. "He knows my swing and my philosophy on hitting. He doesn't involve himself on the mechanics of hitting anymore, however. My dad's more into the mental approach with me now. He helps me with what I am trying to do or what I am looking for. My dad also asks the right questions all the time. For example, he'll ask the question 'What are you doing?' if he thinks I'm grounding out to the second baseman too many times or if I'm popping up too many times. He helps me connect the dots."

The nine-year major-league infielder further explained their relationship with a story and a big smile. "It's funny. One year I was struggling and then one night I went out and got three or four hits. When some reporter after the game asked me what changes I made, I said, 'Last night I talked to my dad and he yelled at me.' After I made that comment I had coaches continually asking me if I had talked to my dad recently. My dad knows what I should be doing and then he challenges me when I'm not doing it. He also reminds me to never get too high or too low."

Lamb was selected by the Texas Rangers out of Cal State Fullerton in the 7th round of the June 1997 draft. He made his major-league debut on Easter Sunday (April 23, 2000) with a start against the Minnesota Twins. His father made it to his debut. "I don't think it really hit him—the impact of me being in that situation—until I got up and hit," Lamb recalled. "It was a good experience having him there."

His father still attends some of his games, "but he gets a little too nervous watching me," Lamb said. "He ends up walking around the stadium a lot. I generally know where he is sitting, and if he's not there I know he's walking around. There are times when I call him and we talk about the game and I'll ask him questions about a certain pitch or an at-bat. And he'd tell me he didn't see it because he was in the left-field pavilion or something like that. He's funny."

His father may talk to him frequently, but he doesn't talk or brag to others about his major-league son. "He's an umpire in California, and a lot of people know him already and know that I'm his son," Lamb explained. "What's funny is that there are a lot of umpires in the big leagues who ask me how my dad is."

With years of input from his father, Lamb has learned a lot from his elder and agreed to share some of that wisdom. "One of the most important lessons I learned from my dad was the ability to learn from my mistakes. It's okay to make errors. It's okay to make mistakes out there in the field. But not learning from them is the big mistake. You will always be in a situation when you can make a wrong decision, but right or wrong, you can always learn something from it."

◆ RYAN LANGERHANS ◆

Ryan Langerhans grew up in Round Rock, Texas, where his father, John, was the coach of the high school baseball team. Ryan was coached by his father while in Little League and on one of his All-Star teams and then all through high school.

John Langerhans was inducted into the Texas High School Baseball Coaches Hall of Fame in February 2007. Son Ryan benefited from his father's experience and, in an amusing story, his popularity. "He might have gotten me out of a traffic ticket because he's kind of well-known where we are from," smiled the six foot three outfielder. "I was pulled over one time. I don't remember what I did wrong. The officer recognized the name because of my dad, so I got off with just a warning."

Having a father with such coaching experience, Langerhans was sure to learn a lot. "How to the play the game is what I remember most about what he instilled in me," said Langerhans. "My dad taught me how to play to win and to play hard all the time. It's a lesson I still follow each and every time I step on the field. He also taught me not to worry about personal situations. By playing hard and playing for your teammates, your stats will be where you want them to be at the end of the season."

"I got called up and my dad was the first person I called when I got the news," said Langerhans. "I was pretty excited that they were able to make it. Playing in a big league stadium and watching me play ball was pretty exciting for him."

In addition to the Braves, he has played for the Oakland Athletics, Washington Nationals, Seattle Mariners, and the Los Angeles Angels of Anaheim. But despite all his major-league experience, Langerhans still turns to his father for advice. "I still talk to him at least twice a week," he said. "We don't talk about baseball all the time. He's respectful of that unless I bring it up . . . most of the time I'll bring it up.

"For example," he continued, "if I go 0 for 4, I'm calling him, and I'm asking him if he saw anything different in my swing. And he's pretty good about that. He'll generally pick out something in my swing that will really help me out. When he was younger he spent some time in the Indians organization. As I was growing up he spent a lot of time throwing batting practice to me and we spent a lot of time just talking about baseball."

◆ ADAM LAROCHE ◆

David Adam LaRoche, more commonly known as Adam LaRoche, grew up around baseball. His father, David, was a pitcher in the major leagues from 1970 through 1983 with the Los Angeles Angels, Twins, Cubs, Indians, and Yankees, but still had time to coach his sons. "He was basically my coach for my whole life," said Adam LaRoche. "He was the only coach I had. There were other coaches and there were other guys on the team my dad played on, but he was the one who taught me everything I know.

"I spent my life around the park," he continued. "It was incredible growing up around it. He was my coach in high school and during my first year in college."

Adam graduated from Fort Scott High School in Kansas in 1998. The Florida Marlins drafted him twice as a pitcher—in 1998 and 1999—but he did not sign. After high school, he went to Fort Scott Community College, where he was coached by his father in 1999. The following year, he transferred to Seminole Junior College in Oklahoma, where he was MVP of the Junior College World Series.

The Atlanta Braves selected him as a position player in the 29th round of the June 2000 draft and he signed. The Braves named him as their starting first baseman prior to the 2004 season—before he had even played a game in the majors.

"My dad was at my first game," recalled LaRoche, of his April 7 MLB debut. "It was Opening Day in 2004 against the New York Mets. I was nervous, but it was probably because it was a dream of mine for so long. It could take you awhile to get used to it, but fortunately, I have been around this lifestyle all my life, so that really helped me to get comfortable being here."

LaRoche said his father not only helped him get comfortable with the major-league atmosphere, he also taught him the best emotional approach to staying in the majors. "The greatest lesson I learned from my dad that still applies today is: don't get too high; don't get too low. Always maintain an even temper. Some days, you're going to go 4 for 4, but tomorrow you might be 0 for 4. If you think you've conquered the world, you won't have the right frame of mind to go out there the next day to help win the ball game for your team," said the six foot three first baseman.

"My dad knew that I had what it took physically and

mechanically to play this game. It's the mental part that is so tough at times that he was so good at. You hear about some guys who have unbelievable talent, but they don't have it upstairs and they are the ones that don't stick around this game very long. It's the guys who have some talent or great talent and have it together upstairs and who are mentally tough, don't let the ups and downs get to them . . . they are the ones that make up the superstars in this game."

◆ MATT LECROY ◆

Matt LeCroy's father coached him in baseball when he was young, but Matt will be the first to point out that his mother was also very involved in his baseball development. "My momma was actually my first coach," LeCroy stated. "I was four years old and played in T-ball. My dad came along by age seven and then all the way up to age eleven."

The South Carolina native got great advice from both parents. "My mom and dad taught me never to give up; if you start something, you better finish it and to play as hard as you can possibly play when you're out there playing. You've got to prove yourself every day.

"They helped teach me what it meant to be a part of a team and the importance of being a part of something special," LeCroy continued. "They drove that into me and it has always helped me a lot. They also taught the importance of hard work and the dedication of how they lived their own lives. They were always an example to me of hard work and being prepared. I have been fortunate to play the game. I am not the greatest athlete, but I make up for it in hard work."

The gregarious catcher shared one of his more vivid memories of playing with his father. "I almost broke my daddy's leg one time and I thought I had ruined him," recalled LeCroy. "He was pitching to me when I was younger and I hit a line drive right back at his leg and it felt like that leg stayed bruised for two years! He always worked hard with me. He never pushed me, but on the other hand he also never let me quit. And again, if I started something, I had to make sure I finished it."

LeCroy was a star catcher at Clemson University when he was selected by the Minnesota Twins in the first round (50th overall) of the June 1997 draft. He had already appeared in the College World Series twice and earned a bronze medal with Team USA at the 1996 Olympics in Atlanta.

He made the Opening Day roster for the Minnesota Twins in 2000 and started their first game, on April 3, against the Tampa Bay Devil Rays. His parents were in attendance for that game. "I was a little nervous, although I had already played in some pretty big games," LeCroy admitted, "but I was just glad my parents were there. You grow up all your life dreaming of playing in the big leagues and you finally make it and that becomes pretty special."

LeCroy's parents are very proud. "My momma goes around telling everyone I'm her son and she's pretty loud," LeCroy shared fondly. "My daddy is pretty quiet and low key. But I can tell he's there."

◆ BRAD LIDGE ◆

Brad Lidge began his athletic career as a soccer player. He was very young and he followed that soccer "career" by playing football, baseball, and basketball. And his father coached him in each of them. "Over the years," Lidge reminisced, "my dad devoted countless seasons to being a coach and it was something I have always appreciated."

Looking back, Lidge realized it was more than just an appreciation he had for his father. "My dad was someone I definitely admired growing up. As for professional sports, I had a lot of favorites in all the sports I played, from baseball to football to basketball, but my dad was definitely first and foremost."

Fortunately for the baseball world, the future All-Star pitcher opted for and excelled in baseball. As a junior at Notre Dame in 1998, he was the Big East Player of the Year and then became the Houston Astros' first selection in the June draft.

The Astros brought him up in April 2002 and Lidge's father rushed to see his debut. "When I got called up my dad flew down to Florida to be there for my first game," Lidge recalled of his April 26 big-league debut. "Unfortunately, I didn't get to throw while I was down there. We then traveled to Atlanta and he followed the team. I got to throw there for my debut and he was there to see it. And it was pretty awesome!"

Lidge's father was proud of his son and remains so to this day. But the younger, humble Lidge had a tough time admitting it with a straight face. "I hope he is," he chuckled. "I think he just might be. Well, at least a little. What I do think is he is one proud dad and I am one proud son."

Lidge, now a father of two, had a unique take on the greatest thing he has learned from his father. "I think the best lesson he taught me was how to interact with your son by preparing me to be a father. Being a dad myself takes a lot of energy, but it's the greatest job and it's rewarding. He was the greatest example I have and he did an amazing job with me for sure . . . and that is something I will always remember."

◆ MIKE LIEBERTHAL ◆

Like all the other Major League Baseball players in this book, Mike Lieberthal was coached by his father. But he received his baseball tutoring from a special vantage point; his father, Dennis, was a Major League Baseball scout (with the San Francisco Giants and Detroit Tigers).

"My dad taught me a lot about baseball of course," said the usually quiet Lieberthal, "but he mostly taught me the concept of hard work and the work ethic."

Lieberthal grew up with baseball and all he wanted to do was play the game. Following his father's advice, he worked hard to reach his goal of playing in the majors.

"I remember a lot of long drives in the car with my dad," Lieberthal recalled. "We used to run around sometimes—me playing in two or three games a day all over the Los Angeles area—and he was always there for me."

Lieberthal was considered too small (five foot four, 155 pounds) to catch for his Westlake High School team, so he usually played second base. However, by the time he was a junior, he switched to catcher at the suggestion of pro scouts, including his father.

The switch proved to be the right move for the Californian when the Phillies selected him with their first pick (3rd overall) of the June 1990 draft. Four years later, he made his major-league debut with the Phillies against his hometown team, the Los Angeles Dodgers. "It was at Dodger Stadium, I was nervous, not because my dad was there, but because it was my first game and I grew up a Dodgers fan," confessed Lieberthal.

The "small" catcher ended up playing for the Phillies from 1994 to 2006 and finished his career with the Dodgers in 2007. Like any other father—and many a scout—Dennis Lieberthal was proud of his No. 1 son. "Early on, he was especially proud," smiled the younger Lieberthal, "and he was even more so after as many years as I had been in this game."

◆ JAMES LONEY ◆

James Loney grew up in Missouri City, Texas, near a baseball stadium. "Balls would sometimes fall in our backyard," said Loney. "When I was little, I'd roll them around and play with them. That is how it all started for me."

It continued with his father coaching him in baseball. "My dad was always there. He was my coach all through my Little League days," explained Loney.

"My dad taught me to work as hard as I can and do my best in whatever I do. And, it wasn't just in baseball, but in all that I do," said the first baseman. "He'd say, 'Always play as hard as you can.'"

Loney graduated from Lawrence E. Elkins High School in 2002. Just prior to graduation, the six foot two athlete was selected by the Los Angeles Dodgers in the first round (19th overall) of the June draft. Accolades poured in following the draft, most notably from *Baseball America*, which dubbed Loney, the "Best Pure Hitter" in the draft.

He paid his dues in the minors and made it to the majors in 2006. His debut was on April 4 against the Braves and he singled in his first MLB at-bat against John Smoltz. "My dad was there for my first game in Los Angeles back in 2006," recalled Loney. "It was fun for me and for him. Knowing my dad was out there helped me to relax and to have a good time."

Loney doesn't see his father every day, but he doesn't need to. "Even though I don't turn to him for advice, I know he is always there for me," explained Loney. "Whenever I do see him, he is always there with positive advice. I know it's always advice I can use and I look forward to it."

◆ EVAN LONGORIA ◆

Evan Longoria, the 2008 American League Rookie of the Year, was a late bloomer.

"My dad was my coach beginning at age five until I was ten or eleven—from T-ball days on up," said Longoria, the oldest of four siblings.

"The greatest lesson he instilled in me was a love for the game of baseball," said the likeable third baseman. "Growing up, my dad always told me that he would never force me to do anything, but rather he would support anything I chose to do . . . and when my love for baseball was pretty obvious at an early age, he was there for me."

It wasn't always fun and games, though, according to Longoria. "I was six or seven, maybe eight years old, and my dad would always get a little upset with me when I pitched and I was doing terribly and I would start crying on the mound. I can just remember him walking out to the mound and him giving me that stern look—almost a yell, but not really—saying, 'What are you doing crying out here?' But he made sure not to go too far with his look because he didn't want me to cry even more," recalled Longoria with a smile.

"We had plenty of those moments," he continued. "I remember he also used to yell at me in the morning on the way to the game because I hated to wear stirrups as a little kid, and we used to wear stirrups with our uniform all of the time. So the two of us would go back and forth all the time about stirrups. It's all fun now thinking back."

The three-time All-Star and two-time Gold Glove winner at third base had no realistic hope of making the majors as a skinny kid who received zero scholarship offers upon graduating from St. John Bosco High School in California. He played for a year at Rio Hondo Community College. There, he attracted the attention of Cal State University, Long Beach, which offered him a scholarship.

"Baseball as a profession didn't become a reality for me until I got to college," said Longoria. "Before that, it was always fun for me . . . and when my dad instilled that love of the game in me early in life, he was there to support me."

The player who did not even get drafted or receive a scholarship offer in 2003 became the 3rd overall selection in the June 2006 draft, thanks to the Tampa Bay Rays and Longoria's designation as the "Best Pure Hitter" in the draft among college players by *Baseball America*.

A confident Longoria rose quickly through the minors and made his major-league debut on April 12, 2008, in a game against the Baltimore Orioles attended by his parents. The likable Longoria has risen from the status of unwanted, to underdog, to a major-league success story on the field (where he's earned spots on the All-Star team in three of his first four seasons) and off the field (where he's gained numerous magazine spreads, endorsement deals, and commercial).

But there is still one constant in Longoria's life, someone who has been with him for the entire journey—his father. "I talk to him often," said Longoria. "Not so much about baseball stuff. I mean, I think he knows that I might know a little bit more about baseball these days than he does. If I do talk about baseball with him it's more mental relief than anything else. It's nice to talk, and to have someone that will listen and is there for me."

◆ MARK LORETTA ◆

David Loretta was an investment banker, which led to his children—including future Major League Baseball player Mark Loretta—spending a few years of their young lives in Mexico. "I remember there was a coach they had where I lived in Mexico who they called 'the Professor.' It wasn't an organized league, but more of a get-together league," recalled Loretta, "and I remember playing baseball with this 'Professor' early on."

The Loretta family returned to the States—Southern California to be exact. It was there that Mark's father did his baseball stint. "My dad did a little bit of everything when I was in Little League," the infielder shared. "Even though he traveled a lot, he helped out whenever he could. He coached, he umpired, he helped out in the concession stand, and he ran the PA system, things like that. He would never miss a game. He used to schedule his traveling around my Little League games. I had a great Little League experience and he was always there to share in it."

Loretta went to St. Francis High School, and then to Northwestern University, where he earned his business degree in organizational studies in 1993. That same year, he was selected by the Milwaukee Brewers in the 7th round of the June draft.

He made his major-league debut two years later, on September 4, 1995. "I was with the Brewers at the time and we played in Minnesota for my debut," explained Loretta, "and my parents were both at the game. I was nervous—not because my parents were there, but because it was my first game. My dad and mom have been with me the whole way down the line. It was really comforting to have them there."

Loretta retired after a nearly fifteen-year Major League Baseball career during which his parents went to see him play as often as possible. "I usually knew where they were sitting," said the two-time All-Star. "My dad loved to move around the stadium. I remember one game while in Boston I spotted him in the front row. I saw him while I was on deck. I got the chance to wave at him, but you never know where he'll end up. But I always do seem to find him."

Looking back, Loretta has gained an even greater appreciation for the way his parents raised him, his brother, and his sister. "My dad has always been a positive influence in my life," said Loretta. "My mom and dad in general were not overwhelming or pushy. They were very supportive. The message to us was always to do your best, then you can't ask for anything more than that. You are going to have ups and downs, in baseball and in life, and it's your character that will determine how you handle it all."

◆ MIKE LOWELL ◆

Mike Lowell, a thirteen-year major-league third baseman, got a jump on his professional career thanks to his dad and to his older brother. "My dad was my coach from about seven until I was about twelve years old. I had a brother who was two years older than me, so I always seemed to be playing one level above what I should have been playing because we were on the same team all the time. It made coaching for my dad so much easier," recalled Lowell.

"Playing at a higher level seemed to benefit me. It helped me mature as a player a little bit faster and quicker. My expectation was a little higher, though, from the standpoint of my father, whether I could handle it or not. Fortunately, I could. My dad wasn't one who pushed me into playing anything I didn't like, but I liked baseball," said Lowell.

"My first memory of baseball wasn't in Little League," said Lowell, "but rather playing baseball in the streets with my dad and me and my brother . . . playing pepper all the time. I remember my dad would always work half days on Wednesdays and we were out there playing all the time. That is something that will forever be stuck in my head. I remember going to the park all the time and he'd hit ground balls and pitch batting practice to us all the time. Then afterward, we'd go to the 7-Eleven and get a Slurpee. It was a special time for me growing up. It certainly was a bonding moment for me and my dad. It's something I know a lot of kids haven't been able to experience. It was a highlight for me each time."

Lowell was born in Puerto Rico, but moved to Miami, Florida, when he was four years old. He graduated in 1991 from Coral Gables High School, where he was All-State in baseball. He went on to Florida International University, where he earned a degree in finance. On the baseball field, he was named All-Conference three times and tallied a .353 career average at FIU. In addition, he was named the Trans-America Athletic Conference's Student of the Year and was an Academic All-American honoree in 1995.

He was selected by the New York Yankees in the 20th round of the June 1995 draft. He made his major-league debut on

September 13, 1998, against the Toronto Blue Jays, singling in his first at-bat. The six foot four third baseman was traded to the Florida Marlins on February 1, 1999, shortly before he was diagnosed with testicular cancer. He underwent surgery and three months later returned to the field.

"The first game my dad attended was on May 29, 1999, my first game for the Marlins," Lowell said matter-of-factly. "But when I was in the minors he used to set aside one week each year and make a trip to see me and watch all the games that week. He saw me play in Greenwich, Connecticut; Tampa, Florida; and Greensboro, North Carolina. It was pretty cool how he saw me at each level and was able to experience my progress."

The father and son still talk a lot. "He had a decent background playing for the Puerto Rican National Team when he was younger," said a proud Lowell. "So he understands a lot of what I go through and the grind of playing this game every day. We don't talk about the mechanics of the game. We do talk about the teams I'm on and how well they are doing. We talk like two guys having a beer at a bar and discussing the way things are. And we enjoy it. I like talking about baseball and so does he, and it's something we both have in common. I remember when I was young and we used to sit around together and watch whatever game was on the television. Growing up, that was pretty cool for me."

Thinking back, Lowell decided the greatest lesson his father taught him was that there was a certain way to play baseball. "You should respect the game and your teammates, but not to fear your opponents and the other players," he said. "I think there is a line at times when people give too much respect to other players because they are superstars or because of their reputation, and that will eventually affect your own playing ability and talents. My dad helped me to understand they are trying to compete against you the same way, but don't be afraid of them.

"My dad used to talk to me about having fun," Lowell continued. "He never talked to me about making it this far or the major leagues at all. My dad would always say, 'You don't have to play baseball, but you do have to do something.' You are not going to sit around the house all day and watch television. Fortunately, I was an active kid and I enjoyed playing sports. My dad also coached me when I played volleyball and he was active when I played basketball. I just enjoyed playing baseball a little bit more than anything else. I was good at it, so it was fun for me."

◆ ROB MACKOWIAK ◆

Sometimes, the long shot comes in and surprises you; such was the case with Rob Mackowiak. Selected by the Pittsburgh Pirates in the 53rd round of the June draft in 1996, he bided his time in the minors, made his major-league debut in 2001, and remained in the big leagues for eight seasons.

His father started to help him make that unlikely journey when he coached Mackowiak in Little League. He remained his son's coach into his early teens. "My dad was always the type of guy who was pretty laid-back," revealed Mackowiak. "He always taught you the right way to play. If you were going to play for him, that meant you were going to play hard and you were going to do the right things on the ball field. The minute you step off in another direction, he was always reminding you what it meant to play hard. For example—run the bases hard and do the right things. If you didn't do these things, he'd say something like, 'Okay, let's go home. We are not going to play anymore.' It is a lesson I follow today. Because of my dad, I play the game right. He was very baseball wise."

The outfielder graduated from Lake Central High School in Indiana in 1994. He then went to South Suburban Junior College for two years before getting drafted by the Pittsburgh Pirates.

Mackowiak continued to play the game right and finally got the call to the big leagues on May 18, 2001. "My dad was there for my first game," he recalled. "It was nice. I actually got called up, but the game was rained out that night. We were in Pittsburgh, so my dad would not have been able to be there if it hadn't been rained out. He made it there the next day and, because of the rain out, he was able to see me play in my first game! It worked out perfectly for him to be there."

Mackowiak said his father's role had changed over the years, but he remained a very important part of his life. "My dad is a very loyal person. He comes out to my games all of the time. I don't turn to him for advice on baseball anymore. However, if I need some mental advice, then I still turn to him."

◆ GREG MADDUX ◆

Greg Maddux was born in Texas, but spent much of his childhood in Spain, where his father, Dave, was stationed.

"My earliest memory of baseball was on the U.S. Air Force base in Madrid, Spain, where my father coached me," said Maddux. "We all wore these dirt-colored uniforms with green caps. I always remember being around my dad playing baseball in the backyard and stuff like that."

Even as a kid, Maddux was highly competitive, a trait it seems he inherited. "My father coached me on my first Little League team. I must have been five or six years old. They needed coaches and he was willing to step up. He told them that he would coach if I didn't have to play T-ball but if I could play Pee Wee ball. So I got to play Pee Wee ball."

Known as "The Professor" during his extraordinarily successful twenty-three-year Major League Baseball career, Maddux said he had a very wise father as his coach. "The greatest lesson I learned from my father was that you've got to think for yourself. You've got to learn how to do things for yourself. I know it was a hard thing for a dad to do and say, but he did it. My father was great," said Maddux.

He continued, "The best baseball advice my dad gave me was when I turned twelve and he said to me, 'Okay, that is all I know, now go and listen to your other coaches.' He totally felt like the other coaches had more knowledge than he did and they should take over coaching me. At that point he stayed completely out of it. He let the other coaches coach. Yet, he was still there every game I played."

In 1984, Maddux graduated from Valley High School in Las Vegas, Nevada, where his family had settled after returning from Spain. The right-handed pitcher was selected by the Chicago Cubs in the 2nd round of the June draft that year.

The four-time Cy Young Award winner made his Major League Baseball debut on September 2, 1986, against the Houston Astros, as a pinch runner, and then pitched the 18th inning, allowing a home run in his lone inning of work.

Maddux made his first major-league start five days later, on September 7, against the Reds. "My first game was in Cincinnati and I was in a Chicago uniform," he recalled. "My father also had ten brothers and sisters that all grew up in the southern Indiana area. We grew up as Reds fans. We were just forty-five minutes from Riverfront Stadium, where the Reds played at the time. So everyone was able to come down and see me play."

Maddux, a sure bet to make the Hall of Fame when he becomes eligible in 2013, still turns to his father for advice, but not regularly, "just occasionally, when the moment comes up for the two of us."

◆ RYAN MADSON ◆

"My dad was my coach all throughout my life," said right-handed pitcher Ryan Madson, "but officially he was considered my coach from ages six to fourteen years old."

The California native reflected on the greatest lesson his father, the coach, taught him. "What he always instilled in me was to have confidence in myself," Madson said. "My dad would always tell me, 'I know you can do it' or 'Don't stress about it.' He would always tell me 'You were born to be a baseball player.'"

Madson graduated from Valley View High School in 1998, the same year his father's prediction became a reality, when the Philadelphia Phillies selected Ryan Madson in the 9th round of the June draft.

Madson made his big-league debut in 2003, with his only appearance of the season, on September 27 against the Atlanta Braves. Since then, he has spent every year in the majors.

"Whenever we get out to the West Coast, my dad has an opportunity to catch a lot of games, because that is where they live," explained Madson. "The first time we were out there, when I was in the big leagues, he didn't get the chance to see me play because I was hurt," recalled Madson of a sprained ligament he suffered in his right hand in 2004.

"Then the next time we were out there, my dad was pumped to see me. He was sitting right near the bullpen in all his Phillies gear, watching me and so excited. Fortunately, I had a great game and it was fun for him. He told me after the game, 'I knew you could do it.'"

Thinking back, Madson recalled another special time his father came to see him play. "When we were in Los Angeles one time, I didn't know he was going to be at the game," Madson explained. "He surprised me. During batting practice, I was shagging fly balls in left field. The music was on in the stadium and it was loud all around and I was in la-la land. My dad was on the right-field line and he just whistled a few times and it pierced my ears. My head snapped around and I said to myself, 'Holy Gosh! Wow! My dad's here!' It was probably one of the best feelings I had on the baseball field. Just knowing he was there and not knowing he was going to come was an awesome experience for me."

The six foot six pitcher and father of three is still in contact with his father on the "other" coast. "I talk to him at least once a week and we talk about all kinds of stuff," said Madson. "He goes on and on. I'll talk to him about a certain pitch if I'm struggling with my curveball for example, and I might be frustrated. Then he'll give me some advice and the next day I'll throw it and it will be perfect. It all goes back to the confidence he gives me. My dad helps me to relax and not worry about the game as much. Worrying is not his way."

Madson is sure his father is proud of him. "My dad never says how he feels, he just exudes confidence," he explained. "My dad is my biggest fan. He tells everybody what I do, but that's cool. If I had a son in the big leagues, I'd be doing the same thing. It was nice to have a dad who wanted to help you and guide you along the way. If I'd had a dad who said 'I don't want to do this' or 'I don't feel like doing this,' then I wouldn't be here today."

◆ JOE MAUER ◆

Joe Mauer has his father, Jake, to thank for much of his continuing baseball success. "My dad was my coach for a few years, but he still calls me when he thinks I'm doing something wrong," said the Minnesota native. "My dad has seen my swing since I was little, so he knows the most about it."

His first baseball memory, however, dated back to before his father coached him. "I can remember T-ball," said the All-Star catcher. "My grandpop was our coach then, making sure everyone had their own spot on the bench. He made sure their hat wasn't in their glove, meaning they were paying attention when they were in the field. It was a nice memory for me."

Mauer said that even though his dad wasn't always his coach, he was always there for him. "If he wasn't coaching, he was always there for the game. Both of my parents worked, so I knew how tough it must have been to make my games," recalled Mauer.

In addition to attending games, Mauer's father worked with all three of his sons at home. To help his sons hit a baseball more consistently, he created a contraption that became known as the "Quickswing," which is now used by numerous colleges, high schools, youth organizations, and professional baseball players. The biggest beneficiary of the "Quickswing"—and of course the biggest promoter of it, due to his success—was Jake Mauer's middle son, Joe.

"My dad taught me a lot about baseball over the years," said the 2009 American League MVP. "For example, he taught me that you're not going to get a hit in every at-bat. That it is a game of failures, but you've got to stick with it and keep working to get better."

Joe was selected by the Minnesota Twins with the very first pick of the June 2001 draft out of Cretin-Derham Hall High School, where he played basketball and football in addition to baseball. He made his major-league debut less than three years later, on April 5, 2004, against Cleveland.

"My dad was there for Opening Night and my first game," said Mauer. "For me, it was pretty cool because I grew up in Minnesota and was always a Twins fan. It was nice to have a lot of my family and friends there to share in my special day."

Joe now has over eight seasons of major-league service under his belt, as well as four All-Star selections, three batting titles, three Gold Gloves, and one MVP. But he still seeks out his dad when he needs direction. "I always turn to him for advice," he said, "and if I don't, he tells me about it. He wants to help me and when things go bad, it's not a bad idea to ask him what might be going on. But whether things go right or wrong, he'll always be my biggest fan!"

◆ BRIAN MCCANN ◆

Sometimes the son you least expect to make it turns out to be the most successful. Such is the case with Howie McCann. His younger son, Brian, has established himself as one of the best catchers in Major League Baseball, even though his older son, Brad, was initially deemed the sure thing in the family.

Brian McCann was selected by the Atlanta Braves in the 2nd round of the June draft when he was a senior at Duluth High School in 2002. He signed and has gone on to be named to six National League All-Star teams. Brad McCann turned down an offer to play in the pros and attended Clemson University, then toiled in the minor leagues for four years after signing with the Florida Marlins in 2004, but never got the break he was looking for.

"I always looked up to my brother and my dad as I grew up," recalled Brian McCann, one of the most caring players in the game. "My best memory growing up was when I competed in the sixteen-year-old World Series. We were all together. My dad was the coach, my brother was the shortstop, and I was behind the plate. It was pretty amazing. It was an awesome experience to get the opportunity to play in such an important game, on the field with your brother and your father. It ranks up there for me as my best baseball memory."

He lived in West Virginia until he was about eleven years old, when he moved to the Atlanta area. "My dad's full-time job when I was growing up was head baseball coach for Marshall University, but he still coached me on my All-Star teams," said McCann. "He taught me everything about the game when I was growing up."

After his college-coaching career, his father, Howie, opened a very popular baseball academy in Atlanta. Brian McCann benefited greatly from his father's knowledge about baseball and about life. "My dad would always say, 'have fun playing.' He never once placed any pressure on me to play or to make a particular play or get this hit. And, I believe it should be like that, but I still had a passion for it. If you get pressured into playing this game, you won't ever want to continue playing this game," mused McCann.

"He taught me how to be a hitter. My dad was always positive. At no time was he ever negative."

His father was there at his younger son's major-league debut on June 10, 2005, against Oakland. The catcher singled in his first at-bat. "He was there for my first game," said McCann. "I was nervous, but not because he was there. All I know was that I was so happy he was there. It was great having him there."

His father is deservedly proud. "He does brag about me all of the time," admitted McCann. "And, it's a thrill for me. I can't imagine how he must feel when he sees me out there."

McCann knows he has an advantage with his dad in the wings. "I talk to him all of the time," he said. "For example, I was struggling recently at the plate and we must have talked for an hour. My dad knows exactly what is going on and what is wrong with my swing. He knows my swing better than anyone."

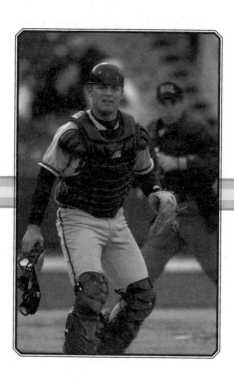

◆ DUSTIN MCGOWAN ◆

Dustin McGowan grew up in Savannah, Georgia. "I remember playing baseball every day when I was a little kid," the right-handed pitcher reminisced. "I'd play at the playground or ball field. It didn't matter where we played as long as it was baseball. We seemed to play all of the time."

His father helped him with his baseball career from the beginning. "My dad was my coach all through Little League up until I was twelve years old," said McGowan. "He taught me to play hard and he helped push me to be the very best that I could. He has probably helped me more than anyone in the game."

Selected out of Long County High School in the first round with the 33rd overall pick by the Toronto Blue Jays in the June 2000 draft, the six foot three pitcher made the jump from Double-A to the majors in 2005. His debut came on July 30 vs. the Texas Rangers.

"It was very memorable," McGowan recalled of his debut. "It was a great moment for us. The game was in Toronto and I flew my dad up on short notice . . . and he was there!

"He is still pretty quiet at times and doesn't want to brag about me," McGowan continued, "but on the inside I know he is very proud and happy."

◆ NATE MCLOUTH ◆

Nate McLouth credits his father with giving him the boost he needed to succeed in the game of baseball. "All the way up to high school, my dad was my coach," said McLouth. "My dad was my coach beginning in T-ball and he continued each step of the way. He was my great motivator and the one who really got me going. He was the person who first put a bat and a ball in my hand. He was always there to have a catch or throw batting practice. My dad would never turn me down if I wanted him to hit grounders or fly balls to me."

McLouth said his father instilled that same dedication in him. "My dad taught me the only way you get where you want to be and, most important, to stay there, was to work hard. He, again, was the best motivator I had. But it didn't stop with him just saying those words; he led by example."

The outfielder was selected by the Pittsburgh Pirates in the 25th round of the June 2000 draft. "I remember when I first played in Low-A ball in Hickory, North Carolina, and my dad was there. My parents and brother were there to see my first home run that day. It was pretty cool! I hit it in their honor. My dad was even there when I made my big-league debut in Washington," recalled McLouth of his June 29, 2005 MLB debut with the Pirates.

McLouth still gets a boost from his father. "Even today, my dad is always there to help me stay positive," he said, "especially when things are not always going well."

Looking back, the Michigan native recalled his first childhood baseball memory. "It was probably first Tigers game. I must have been seven or eight years old at that time. We would go to one game each season and it was always the best day of the year for me," he exclaimed.

"Having my dad around the baseball field with me all my life has been the most positive experience of my life."

◆ DOUG MIENTKIEWICZ ◆

Doug Mientkiewicz was fortunate enough to have his father involved in his baseball career at a young age, and the lessons he learned stuck with him and helped him achieve some rare successes in baseball. He is one of very few players to have won an Olympic gold medal (in 2000, in Sydney, Australia) and earn a World Series title (in 2004, with the Red Sox).

"My dad always had a blue-collar approach to whatever he did," said Mientkiewicz. "So hard work was probably the most important lesson he stressed to me. He'd say, 'Work hard every day and good things will happen.'

"He was my coach all the way up," Mientkiewicz continued. "My dad is still my coach. He watches and TiVos every game I'm in. He then writes down what he thinks I'm doing wrong. It's almost psychotic. But once I had a son of my own I understood it, too. I totally get it now."

Mientkiewicz recalled one of his first baseball memories that exemplified his father's devotion. "I broke my leg one year and my dad modified this lawn chair and the thing a mechanic lays down on when they roll under your car. My dad was then able to throw me ground balls and I could hit without having to favor the broken leg."

The infielder graduated from Westminster Christian High School in Florida a year ahead of someone named Alex Rodriguez. He learned a lot just from watching the future All-Star, who was bigger and stronger than everyone else, and still admires Rodriguez to this day.

Mientkiewicz, however, achieved his own success. He was drafted by the Toronto Blue Jays in 1992 as a high school senior, but elected to attend Florida State University. He was drafted again, by the Minnesota Twins, in the 5th round of the June draft in 1995, and made his Major

League Baseball debut in September 1998. What followed were his Olympic and World Series experiences—the highlights of a solid career.

But his crowning moment in life came in 1995, when he and his wife, Jodi, had their first child, a son. "My dad was a hard-working blue-collar man," Mientkiewicz reiterated. "He'd work all day and then come home and have time to be a good father. That was inspiration and it rubbed off on me. I hope I'll be half the father my dad was."

◆ BENJIE MOLINA ◆

Benjie Molina is the oldest of three brothers, all of them catchers in the major leagues.

His father, Benjamin Sr., played in Puerto Rico's Superior League for fifteen years before retiring from baseball to coach his sons. "My father sacrificed his life for our lives and dreams," Benjie said with heartfelt sincerity. "He used to start work very early in the morning. This way he could be home by four o'clock in the afternoon, and by five o'clock we were at the stadium working out. That tells you that he didn't have his own life. He gave up his life and dreams for us, and lived every day for us. That is the best advice I have for other fathers out there . . . to live for your children. I had a great dad!"

The Gold Glove catcher reminisced about the "old" days back in Vega Alta, Puerto Rico. "My dad was my coach from age five on up. Back then we used to call it the 'Pampers League' when you are that young," said Molina.

"I have a picture of me pitching with one of my uniform pant legs up and the other uniform pant leg down. Everybody started to laugh at me, but I didn't know the difference. I was six years old and fashion wasn't a big thing for me."

Benjie credits his father for a lot of his success. "My brothers and I learned so many things from my father. It's hard to say just one thing," said Benjie. "I think the biggest thing he helped us to learn is desire, determination, the passion, work ethic, and the respect for the game. It's all the little things you have to do and understand to become a great person. I can't point to one thing he taught us as being more important than the rest . . . he taught us all of these things."

Although Benjie is the oldest, he was not the first Molina brother to catch. Jose, the middle brother, was the first to claim that position. Benjie, originally a pitcher and outfielder, switched positions when a scout said he would give him a tryout if he could catch.

Benjie and his brothers are also the only trio of brothers to each win a World Series championship ring. In fact, the day that Benjie and Jose were playing in game seven of the 2002 World Series, their father Benjamin Sr. was being inducted into the

Puerto Rican Amateur Baseball Hall of Fame—a proud day for the entire Molina family.

Benjie still seeks his father's advice. "We'd talk as often as we could. He's the type that will leave you alone for a little bit and see what you are doing, but the moment he knows you're struggling, he'll call and talk to you about it," said Benjie. "He is not the type of person who calls you all of the time and tells you what you should do. He was always very straightforward with you. He taught us the game. But he also understands this is a different level we all play right now . . . how we played back then is so much different than in the big leagues we play in now. He leaves us alone, but whenever he does call, it is for something good and it has a purpose."

Benjamin Molina, Sr., the proud and loving father of Benji, Jose, and Yadier died in October 2008, doing what he loved. Benjamin Molina's heart gave out while he attended a baseball game during a youth league doubleheader in Puerto Rico. It was the same field where he taught his three sons the game of baseball.

◆ JOSE MOLINA ◆

Jose is the middle brother of the Molina trio of brothers, all of them major-league catchers.

He grew up in Vega Alta, Puerto Rico, with his brothers, Benjie and Yadier, playing baseball every day. "We learned about baseball and the game from my dad," said Jose. "He taught us about everything. My dad was my coach and he was my everything. He taught me the great lessons of life."

Growing up in a soccer-crazy country, baseball took a second seat. But the Molinas preferred baseball and their idol, Roberto Clemente. "He's almost everyone's idol when you ask a player from Latin America," admitted Jose. "When I got to be fourteen or fifteen years old, I started to follow some of the great catchers in the game: Ivan Rodriguez, Sandy Alomar, and Benito Santiago. They were the players I was always looking to follow."

Because Jose was stockier than his older brother, Benjie, he gravitated to the catching position first, and his brothers ended up following suit. "My best [quality] is defense," said Jose. "Defense is what got me here. I work every day on my hitting, but defense is my strength."

Benjie was signed as an amateur free agent by the California Angels in May 1993. Jose was selected by the Chicago Cubs the following month in the 14th round of the June draft. The brothers made it to the majors in consecutive years—1998 for Benjie and 1999 for Jose.

"Our family had always been poor," said Jose. "So early on it was difficult for my dad to come here from Puerto Rico to see me play. I know other players had their fathers up with them right away to see them play, but it was a few years before he came up and had the chance to see me play in person for the first time.

"I was so happy for my parents to see me. I know, and they knew, that all of the hard work they did paid off," revealed Jose.

"My dad is so proud. I know that he is quiet in life, but on the inside, I know that in his heart he is cheering for all of us."

Like his brothers, Jose regularly turns to his father for advice. "In life, it is not easy," said Jose. "My dad is a lot older than me, so he knows. He has always been there to give advice when I have a problem. I am always happy to talk to him and he is always awesome."

◆ YADIER MOLINA ◆

Yadier Molina is the youngest of a unique set of brothers. All three Molinas—Benjamin Jr., Jose, and Yadier—are major-league catchers. He credits their father (and mother) for getting them started on the road to Major League Baseball.

They grew up in Vega Alta, a small rural town in north-central Puerto Rico. After a ten-hour shift at a factory, their father, Benjamin Sr., would hurry home, eat quickly, and grab his glove to play baseball with his boys.

"My father was my first manager," said Yadier, "My dad loves baseball and he taught me to respect the game."

Remembering back to those days in Vega Alta, Yadier happily recalled his first baseball memory. "I was five years old," he said. "We used to call it the 'Pampers League' or the 'Diaper League' because we were all so young and still babies. I remember hitting a home run and my father was waiting for me at home plate, but my pants were falling down because they were too big. I wanted to stop, but my dad said, 'keep going' and when I got to home plate he gave me the biggest hug!"

It was inevitable that Yadier would become a catcher after he watched both of his older brothers play the position. He would pick up their equipment and try it on, . . . and also pick up many tips from them on how to play the position.

He was selected by the St. Louis Cardinals in the 4th round of the June 2000 draft and joined his two MLB brothers when he made his major-league debut on June 3, 2004. "I was the last of my brothers to make it to the big leagues. It was in 2004 and my father was the proudest guy around. He has to be proud because he had two sons already in the major leagues, and then, when I came around, he was even happier," said Molina.

"My father was at my first game. It was in Pittsburgh and it's where I got my first hit. My dad was so excited. He was jumping up and down. It was a great moment for him."

"He makes me feel so proud," Yadier said with profound sincerity.

"I still ask him for advice all the time," Yadier revealed, "and he is always there for me. He watches all the games and I talk to him after every game. I tell him what I did wrong and he is there to talk with me and help."

◆ JUSTIN MORNEAU ◆

Canadian native Justin Morneau has had a very good major-league career already. The six foot four first baseman has won the 2006 American League Most Valuable Player award, gained two Silver Slugger honors, and been selected to four All-Star teams. But it all started with Wiffle ball.

"My earliest baseball memory was playing Wiffle ball in the backyard with my older brother," Morneau recalled. "We played all of the time together. I remember each summer we used to go and play and hit all day and play baseball. We'd go to the park and practice. We used to hit and hit all day and we'd have a lot of fun. And that is when the concept of working hard first came into play."

Morneau's father, George, owned a sporting goods store in New Westminster, British Columbia, where the family lived. He was a hitting coach for many baseball and softball teams, including his sons' teams. "My dad has been my coach pretty much my whole life," Morneau stated.

"My dad always kept it simple," Morneau said of the most important advice he received from his father. "He always stressed to me the importance of working hard at whatever you do."

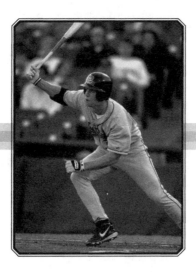

◆ MATT MORRIS ◆

During his major-league career, All-Star pitcher Matt Morris played for three teams—the St. Louis Cardinals, San Francisco Giants, and Pittsburgh Pirates. For the eleven-year major leaguer, however, it all began in his crib. "Knowing my dad the way I do, there was probably a ball and a bat in my crib," mused Morris. "I have always been around those two things."

He grew up in Montgomery, New York. "Little League was great," Morris remembered. "I can remember those Little League days so vividly. I loved watching the Little League World Series. Even today, that is baseball in its purest form and that is refreshing."

Morris said his father enjoyed the Little League experience as much as he did. "You know, my dad did it all," he said. "He was a first-base coach, third-base coach, he'd pick up kids, he'd carpool. . . . My parents were both heavily involved in what I had going on. They made a point of being there and getting me where I had to go. Today, it's a little different. The travel is so crazy. Parents today even get on planes."

Communicating with his father is "a never-ending process," Morris stated matter-of-factly. "He still gives me great advice. He is also the man I have always looked up to in my life. Anytime something goes wrong, he knows me the best. So I can call him to get his advice. I'll admit, I don't always take it—I think I have a better way, but that isn't always the case or true. But I can always count on him being in my ear."

◆ MARK MULDER ◆

Left-handed pitcher Mark Mulder has great hitting and defensive memories from his early baseball days. "I remember a lot of times going out in the backyard and hitting with that big, chunky baseball bat. I remember the first time I hit the ball over the house . . . it rolled down in the front yard and I had to run around and get it. Those are some of my first memories that still feel pretty cool today," he said.

"I remember being a kid and playing T-ball and hitting the ball and running the bases," Mulder continued. "I actually got on the WGN News in Chicago where I'm from when I was a kid because I played center field and turned an unassisted triple play when I was seven or eight years old. It happened when a player hit a line drive and I caught it and then I ran in and stepped on second and then tagged the guy running from first. We were so young nobody knew half the rules anyway. It's funny, but I guarantee you my dad still has the video somewhere. I'll have to see it again for a good laugh!"

Mulder's father coached him, but more than anything, was just there for his son. "He was my head coach when I turned thirteen. I was in the Babe Ruth League, but that was really the only year he coached me," said Mulder. "He always helped out as much as he could when the other coaches needed help. But again, he was always there. He wanted me to have fun and just enjoy the game."

The pleasant and talkative All-Star recalled what he learned from his supportive father: "Patience, I think more than anything. I'm not that person you are going to see jump up and down on the field, or I'm not that person you'll see throwing or breaking things. My dad taught me to be even tempered.

"There are things in this game that are going to jump up and get you. I'm not going to be that person that will get too excited because the very next time things can dramatically go right downhill for you. The highs and lows in this game can be pretty extreme.

"My father taught me to just go out there and do your thing, play hard and have fun," the father of two continued. "And like any father should remember, just enjoy the game and have fun with it."

Mike Mussina was a five-time All-Star pitcher who won seven Gold Gloves and 270 games for the Baltimore Orioles and New York Yankees during an eighteen-year career that may well gain him induction into the Hall of Fame. But he started, like so many others, playing baseball as a kid.

"My earliest baseball memory," recalled Mussina, "was playing Wiffle ball in my backyard. I was very young and I was probably trying to imitate whatever player I just saw on the television.

"I grew up in Pennsylvania and I remember watching the Mets and the Yankees in the mid-seventies and that was my first experience that I remember about baseball and for me paying attention to the game. I can even remember watching the Yankees in 1976 getting swept by the Cincinnati Reds in the World Series and then winning it all the next year against the Dodgers."

Mussina's father coached him when he was eleven and twelve years old. The savvy right-hander learned a lot from his father, but said choosing the most important lesson he picked up from his dad was nearly impossible. "I know I learned a lot of lessons, some so small you don't even remember. Baseball ends up teaching you a lot, and because he got me involved in the game and kept me interested in it and taught me everything he could teach me, then he has taught me a lot," Mussina analyzed. "Baseball teaches you about teamwork and competition, overcoming failures, and all kinds of things.

"My dad always told me there is going to be someone better than you," Mussina continued. "So I would use that statement to keep me motivated. Just when you think you're pretty good at something, I would think of that statement as a way to try even harder."

The astute pitcher opted to go to Stanford University instead of signing with the Baltimore Orioles after they had drafted him in the 11th round in 1987. The move paid off, as he ended up with a degree in economics from a prestigious university and was selected again by the Orioles in 1990, this time in the first-round as the 20th overall selection.

Mussina made his Major League Baseball debut a year later—on August 4, 1991, in Chicago against the White Sox, then his home debut in Baltimore five days later. "My first big-league game was on the road, so the first game my parents saw me play in was my debut at home," he said.

"My parents and brother were there. I didn't last as long as I wanted to in that first game," he said with a wry grin, recalling getting pulled after pitching just over three innings, "but they saw me. And over the years, they've gotten to see me many times since then. They've seen their share, but my father honestly tells me he can't sit for the game. He has to get up or step away from it because he gets too nervous. My brother and mother, on the other hand, wish they could go all of the time."

Mussina was born in Williamsport, home of the Little League World Series, and he still lives in the area with his wife, Jana, and their two sons. He stays busy in the sport, serving on the Little League Board of Directors.

He also still turns to his father for advice. "Not so much on a baseball level, but more about being a dad. I still respect him as my father and try to remember that he will always be your parent and not just a friend. I still look at my father as my father. I'm a father myself and I know it's a lot more work than being a son. I appreciate my dad teaching me what he has taught me over the years and baseball is just a small part of it all."

WES OBERMUELLER

Pitcher Wes Obermueller grew up in America's heartland in Cedar Rapids, Iowa—not far from Dyersville, Iowa, which provided the setting for the film, *Field of Dreams*. He was a stereotypical Midwestern boy, growing up on a farm with a solid family life. "My parents have been active in my life since I was a kid and that goes for baseball," said Obermueller.

"My dad has always played baseball with me since I was five years old," he stated. "I grew up on a farm in Iowa. I remember playing ball in the backyard all of the time. When I first got into organized baseball at our recreation department, no one would step up to be the coach, but my dad knew I wanted to play baseball, so he offered to give it a go."

As a coach, Obermueller's father offered his son advice that ended up sticking with him throughout his career and life. "My dad would always say, 'When you are hitting, be aggressive, and when you are having a catch, keep your eye on the ball,'" recalled Obermueller. "He also taught me to apply this same principle to the game of life—be aggressive, play and work hard, and always go after what you want. But that's what farm life is all about. It's about the work ethic and the harder you work, the greater the payoff. Play hard and things will fall your way."

Obermueller said his father's advice has helped him keep things in perspective, including his father's advice. "My dad likes to give advice, but he knows there are some limitations," he said with a smile. "He is good with that. You know you can turn to your father for all kinds of advice, it's not as much about baseball anymore, but he can still be competitive with you. Your parents always want you to do well and if things are going bad, they are always there for support. They can be critical at times, but always in a good way. I like to think your folks help you stay straight and remind you what you should be doing. Dad has certainly never pampered me, but I wouldn't want it any other way."

Obermueller always played as an outfielder until his senior year at the University of Iowa (where he earned a degree in commercial recreation). It was then that he was selected, as a pitcher, by the Kansas City Royals in the 2nd round of the June 1999 draft.

He made his Major League Baseball debut just over three years later. "I got called up when I was in Kansas City and I got to pitch in my first game in 2002 against the Cleveland Indians, and my parents were there," recalled Obermueller of his September 20 big-league debut. "I was really nervous, but I think my dad was even more nervous than I was. It was a lot of excitement for him and my mom."

◆ LYLE OVERBAY ◆

Lyle Overbay is a first baseman and a fan favorite who has played for four different Major League teams. His father, however, is the reason he is even playing the game.

His father was his coach all through Little League and Babe Ruth League baseball. "My dad always kept things simple for me," said Overbay. "He would always say, 'Watch the ball, make contact, and hit the ball.' It was the best advice he could have given to anybody. My dad was always a baseball guy, but he had other commitments when he grew up, so he wasn't able to pursue a career in the game. My dad has always taught me to enjoy the game. There was never any pressure to play baseball. He's why I play the game!"

The Washington native graduated from Centralia High School in 1995, where he played basketball, football, baseball, and golf. He then attended the University of Nevada, Reno, and was finally selected by the Arizona Diamondbacks in the 18th round of the June 1999 draft.

The Diamondbacks' Minor League Player of the Year in 2001, Overbay made his major-league debut on September 19 of that year. He bopped back and forth between the majors and minors until becoming a full time first baseman in 2003. After being traded to the Milwaukee Brewers prior to the 2004 season, his career really took off.

"My dad is quite proud of me," Overbay stated. "He's funny about it though. I know he is always on eBay buying all of my baseball cards. But he enjoys it!"

He continued, "My dad is always pretty quiet. There was only once that he said anything about me getting it going. I was in A-ball and I had a batting average of only .240 in the month of April. In the beginning of May he called me and said, 'I think it is time to get it going.' I think he knew that I knew a lot about the game, but that was what I needed and I eventually got it going!"

◆ JONATHAN PAPELBON ◆

Jonathan Papelbon was coached by his father "from age eight through fourteen years old. It was Dizzy Dean Little League," said the younger Papelbon. "He actually coached me all the way up to high school."

The right-handed reliever actually started out as a hitter and first baseman. "I remember once moving up to this big barrel bat," Papelbon recalled. "I must have been thirteen or fourteen years old and my dad was throwing me batting practice in the cage. I was hitting horrible because I had changed bats. But then, I drove one back and hit him right in the leg. He had this big fat bruise on his leg, but he was SO proud I hit it!"

Papelbon continued hitting, playing first base, and spot pitching at Bishop Kenny High School in Jacksonville, Florida. After graduating he went to Mississippi State University, also as a first baseman. It wasn't until his second or third year in college that he fully committed to pitching.

Papelbon was selected by the Boston Red Sox in the 4th round of the June 2003 draft. After being named their minor-league Pitcher of the Year in 2004 while with Sarasota (A), he made brief stops at the Red Sox Double-A and Triple-A affiliates before making his major-league debut in July 2005, in a start against the Minnesota Twins—the first of just three starts he made that year and in his career. "Both my parents came up to Fenway Park for the game and they were completely overwhelmed by the Boston atmosphere and everything that goes along with it," recalled Papelbon.

A young pitcher on a fast track raises a lot of expectations from die-hard Red Sox fans. Advice he received from his father continues to help him succeed to this day. "The biggest thing I learned from my dad was on those days that I struggled," the four-time All-Star shared. "He always reminded me to have confidence in myself. He would remind me that everyone struggles and nobody is perfect. And, if you do have a bad day . . . forget about it. 'Put it behind you,' he'd say and 'chalk it up to experience.'"

Papelbon said he continues to gain valuable insights from his father. "I still turn to my dad for advice all of the time with little things here and little things there. Of course my parents know that I am on my own now, experiencing my own thoughts and feelings about everything in life. But when I need him, he is always there for me with open arms."

◆ CARL PAVANO ◆

Carl Pavano has been pitching in the majors since 1998. His professional career began when he was selected by the Boston Red Sox in the 13th round of the June 1994 draft out of Southington High School in Connecticut. He was traded to the Montreal Expos with Tony Armas for Pedro Martinez in November 1997.

The pitcher made his Major League Baseball debut on May 23, 1998, against the Philadelphia Phillies in Montreal and in front of his family. "My entire family was there," said Pavano. "It was a special time for me and my family. Whether things are going good or bad, they have always been there for me. It's been that type of support my entire career. They have given me great memories."

His family's support of his baseball career began when he was still young, according to Pavano. "My dad was my coach in Little League, Babe Ruth League, and all the way up to high school. It was always great having his support all those years."

Looking back, Pavano confessed it was not always hearts and roses. "My dad was pretty hard on me. I don't think he paid me many favors because I was his son. There certainly was never any favoritism.

"The best lesson he taught me," the right-hander continued, "was the importance of the work ethic. That was always big with him. He himself has always been a hard worker, yet he was always there for me!"

Pavano is now a 15-year major leaguer. He's been a National League All-Star, played in the postseason three times, and earned a World Series title in 2003 with the Florida Marlins. He has become a father himself with the births of his son and daughter in 2008 and 2009. But he still turns to his parents for advice. "That is what parents are for," Pavano grinned. "They are the two people in your life you can definitely trust."

◆ JAKE PEAVY ◆

"I can honestly remember I was a small child going to sign up for T-ball," recalled 1997 National League Cy Young Award winner Jake Peavy. "I can remember going to my first practice, going to my first game, and wearing my uniform for the first time. I still have all of the pictures from that year and obviously, that is where the love of the game developed for me, even way back then."

The native of Mobile, Alabama, credits his dad with helping foster that affection for baseball. "I can remember as far back to when I was real young and my father was always real involved and he was always in the coaching role.

"I've learned a lot from my father, without a question," Peavy stated. "I came from a middle-class, blue-collar family, and he certainly taught me about hard work. I remember my mom and dad struggling to provide and seeing the time they spent and the hours they worked and the way they went about their business and always having time for the family. I learned through hard work you can achieve your goals and succeed in life no matter what you do. It rubbed off on me and this is what I learned most from my father."

Peavy went 44–1 in four years at St. Paul's Episcopal High School and in his senior year was selected by the San Diego Padres in the 15th round of the June 1999 draft.

"I think me and my dad are a lot alike," Peavy revealed. "I remember my high school days when you think you have to be a little rebellious. You think you're a man and I remember talking back to my mom a couple of times. My dad was quick to get on me. As I came through those high school days, I gained a tremendous amount of respect for my dad and we eventually become closer. Even today, my dad and I are very tight and we speak almost every other day."

Peavy, a six foot one strike-out pitcher, was called up to the Padres on June 22, 2002, to make his first start in San Diego against the New York Yankees and in front of 60,021 people—the biggest crowd in the majors that year. "It was pretty special," he recalled. "It was my major-league debut. I was pretty young and it was special for my family. It was against the Yankees and I was in San Diego. It was an obvious cool experience especially for my dad who was my coach all of my life growing up and he was able to see it come full circle.

In addition to winning the National League Cy Young Award in 2007, Peavy has been named to two NL All-Star teams. But he's an even bigger All-Star to his three sons, Jacob, Wyatt, and Judson. Being a dad has invested Peavy with a new perspective on parenting, and an even greater esteem for his own mother and father.

"Your parents are so wise and full of wisdom, how can I not turn to my dad for advice?" asked Peavy. "The older I get, the more I know I've learned about life from my dad and mom. They have been in this world and have done and seen and heard more than I have. And, obviously, being a dad, too, there are a lot of challenges that life can bring so it only makes sense for me to turn to them for advice as much as I can. Who better to lean on than my father? I feel like I was raised in a respectable manner, in the right way, and that is why I want to do the same with my kids. My dad has been, and will be, a big influence in my life to this day."

♦ ANDY PETTITTE ♦

One of the most quietly successful pitchers in Major League Baseball history has to be left-hander Andy Pettitte. He got his start, like so many others, with his dad as his baseball coach.

After his family moved to Houston, Texas, from Baton Rouge, Louisiana, when Pettitte was eight, his father became his coach for six years. "My dad loves the game of baseball," Pettitte explained. "Growing up he showed me an awful lot of attention. He was always there for me. He made himself available to me. Every day I'd come home from school and he'd come out and play catch with me. He bought all the stuff that I needed to play—even a portable pitching mound that we used in our backyard."

The three-time All-Star and five-time World Series champion was given advice by his father that has stuck with him. "I can always remember my dad telling me that nobody in the world is going to give me anything and that if I want it, I'm going to have to work for it," recalled Pettitte. "That is the biggest thing that sticks out in my head that he told me."

Pettitte has been in the majors for more than fifteen years and is known for his calmness and determination. He has rarely shown—or admitted to—nervousness. However, one of his rare battles with nerves came when he was making his first major-league start on May 27, 1995. "I was definitely nervous," Pettitte confessed. "My dad was there for my first start, but not my first appearance." he explained. "I made my first start out in Oakland against the A's and he came out and made it to my first start."

After nine years with the Yankees, Pettitte returned home, signing with the Houston Astros in 2004. "It was nice coming home," he reflected. "My dad was at every game. He and my mom were there to support me."

"He always had plenty of advice for me," Pettitte smiled. "Obviously at this stage in my career you listen to what he has to say. I know pretty much at this point when I make mistakes, and when the ball is not doing what I want it to do. But my mom and dad are still there to this day when I have my bad starts and are there to support me and pick me up."

Pettitte, a father of four (three sons and a daughter), knows his father is proud of how far he's come in the game. "Oh yeah, he sure is proud!"

◆ ANDY PHILLIPS ◆

There are a lot of nice guys playing the game of baseball and one of the nicest is Andy Phillips. He credits his father—his assistant coach for his first six years of organized baseball—with providing the lessons that made him the man he became.

"I remember my dad always saying, 'If you are going to start something, just make sure you are there to finish it and complete it the right way,'" recalled Phillips. "I remember starting things when I was younger and then I got to thinking that I might not finish this whole thing . . . and then I'd remember his words. He also spoke about being a man of your word and that had a lot to do with starting and finishing what you needed to do. They were huge lessons for me growing up."

The Tuscaloosa, Alabama, native enjoyed having his father as his coach. "I especially remember when I first started playing baseball I was in this coach-pitch league and my dad was the guy who was always throwing to me," Phillips shared. "That was always fun for me. And, to be there with your dad, at that age, was something special. It was a lot of fun, but I do remember being a little intimidated and afraid he might throw one high and tight," Phillips said with a grin.

The infielder was selected by the New York Yankees in the 7th round of the June 1999 draft out of the University of Alabama. He entered the history books by hitting a home run in his first Major League Baseball at-bat with the Yankees, on September 14, 2004, over the big Green Monster in Boston.

Now a hitting coach for the Alabama Crimson Tide, Phillips recalls those early days of his major-league career with his family. "I can certainly remember the first game my dad attended in the big leagues, but more important I can remember the first day I was called up to the big leagues," said Phillips, recalling August 13, 2004. "My dad and family were all there to share in my news. Actually, I was playing golf with my dad the day before and the next day I got called up . . . and for me to be able to share that time with him on those two special days will always be special for me."

◆ MIKE PIAZZA ◆

Mike Piazza was a major-league catcher for nearly sixteen years, a National League Rookie of the Year in 1993, and a twelve-time All-Star. But as a draft pick in the 62nd round (a round usually filled with marginal prospects and favor picks), he was considered a long shot to step foot in the majors. Piazza beat the odds, however, thanks to a lot of hard work and diligence.

He grew up in Phoenixville, Pennsylvania, the second of five boys. His father, Vincent, worked hard at a young age to give his family a comfortable living. Vincent Piazza earned his money through car dealerships and real estate, but his true love was (and still is) baseball. When he noticed his second son had some baseball ability, he made sure he worked with him and gave him everything he would need to succeed. The knock on Piazza throughout his early career was that he was handed everything, but the reality was (and still is), you can't buy ability and passion.

When Piazza was eleven years old, his father bought him a backyard batting cage. "He gave me the batting cage, but *he* couldn't make me use it," said Piazza, who said he got hooked on baseball through practicing in the cage. "I used the batting cage religiously. Every year, I could feel myself getting better. That was addicting for me."

Five years later, Piazza received another gift, a gift like no other—a private hitting session with the great Ted Williams. The session was videotaped and Piazza has a copy of it to this day. On the tape, Williams sincerely complimented the ability of the visibly nervous Mike Piazza, gave him a few pointers, and finished with, "I guarantee you, this kid will hit the ball. I never saw anybody who ever looked better at his age. But it's only 50 percent of the battle, what he showed me out there."

It wasn't until he watched the tape again, after his first taste of the major leagues in 1992, that Piazza admitted, "Now I know exactly what he was talking about."

At Phoenixville Area High School, Piazza found success playing baseball; he was named the league MVP as a hard-hitting first baseman. But the local acclaim was not enough to get him drafted in his senior year in 1986. That didn't happen until 1988, when Los Angeles Dodgers manager (and Piazza godfather)

Tommy Lasorda selected him out of Miami-Dade Community College with the Dodgers' final pick of the draft.

Lasorda advised his godson to give up first base and switch to catcher to give himself a better chance to reach the big leagues. The godson did as directed, switching positions and continuing to work and pay his dues in the Dodgers' minor-league system. He finally reached the majors in September 1992. "I was lucky to have the opportunities," Piazza admitted, "but I did the work."

Still, Piazza advises young players not to let their hard work on baseball undermine their enjoyment of the game. "Always remember to have fun playing baseball with your friends and teammates," he said. "That really is where the camaraderie starts with baseball."

Piazza said he has many fond memories of playing baseball during his formative years. "I still remember all the fun I had in Little League," said Piazza. "I am a big fan of Little League and how it helps you to become a better person. It was where the seeds were kind of planted for me and the desire to become a major-league player one day. Not every Little Leaguer can go on to become a major leaguer, which is why it is so important to just enjoy the experience. It is a good time to enjoy social interaction with other kids, to learn how to be competitive, and to learn the concept of good sportsmanship."

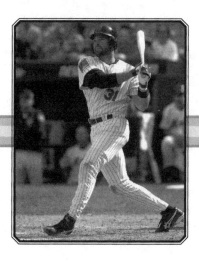

◆ SCOTT PODSEDNIK ◆

Not every player rides the fast track to the major leagues. For some, like outfielder Scott Podsednik, the journey can take years, but the time spent and lessons learned in the minors can make the taste of success in the majors all the more savory.

"I think that being successful is about how you deal with the hard times," said Podsednik. "The people who can deal with set-backs are the people who can continue to move forward. I definitely learned what it takes to grind through some of the tough times."

Podsednik, whose father coached him in summer leagues until he got to high school, graduated from West High School (Texas) in 1994. The track and baseball star had college offers, but when he was selected by the Texas Rangers in the 3rd round of the draft that June, he opted to begin a professional baseball career.

The young Texan, who had never been far away from home, toiled in minor-league towns all over the country with the Rangers and Florida Marlins organizations before joining the Seattle Mariners organization in November 2000. He made his major-league debut the following year, on June 5, 2001, but didn't firmly establish himself as a major leaguer until 2003, with the Milwaukee Brewers.

"My dad was at my first game. It was in Los Angeles. I didn't get an at-bat, but he was still there," said the soft-spoken Podsednik. "He flew up from Texas to see me, and he was sure proud. No question about it!"

He continued, "I still call my dad and we talk about the game. He watches all the games and he has certainly seen me progress as a player. He has seen me play this game throughout my entire career. So every now and again I give him a buzz and ask him if he's seen anything different in my level of play."

Podsednik said his father taught him the lesson that helped him eventually reach his dream. "He told me just to go out and play hard every day," Podsednik said reflectively. "He would say, 'You've been given some wonderful abilities to play this game, so go out there and play the game hard. If you do this every day, then things will take care of themselves.'"

◆ CLIFF POLITTE ◆

Right-hander Cliff Politte had some big shoes to fill as he was growing up. "My father was my coach for the majority of my Little League days. He played professional baseball in the St. Louis organization, and he had a lot of great baseball knowledge. So, he coached me on many of my Little League teams."

His father was a good coach, but they still had one significant difference. "He was a left-handed pitcher and I'm a righty," explained Politte. "He always did the best he could, and I do know that I would not have been a big leaguer without some of the stuff he taught me."

He continued, "I used to call my dad after every game I pitched. Good or bad we talked. If it was bad, I knew I had someone I could complain to or help me get it off my shoulders. We talked about pitches and how I could do better next time. I remember struggling one time and I couldn't figure it out, so I called my dad. He said I was mixing my pitches well, but it was all about location. I went back to look at the tapes, and he was right. I had to remember each time he did that, that it wasn't his first rodeo, he had done it all before."

The Missouri native credits has father for giving him the most important advice of his career. "Never give up. I know there were a couple of times I wanted to quit. I remember playing outfield and all the other positions. He'd throw batting practice with me every day, and there were days I just didn't want to go out there. There were times I'd be in the car before a game or practice and I'd say 'No.' But my dad was always encouraging me and the next day I'd be back in the batting cage with him. He taught me to never give up."

Politte graduated from Vianney High School where he was captain of both the baseball and soccer teams. He went on to Jefferson Junior College where he was an All-American baseball player. However, the five foot four pitcher was not selected in the June draft until the 54th round in 1995, when the St. Louis Cardinals took a chance on him.

He quickly showed promise and made it to the majors with his debut on April 2, 1998. "It was the season's second game in St. Louis," Politte recalled. It was a day game and they shut down my high school and everyone went—my family and my friends, they were all there. It was a very special moment. It was overwhelming for me."

Prior to that game, Politte did something special for his dad. "I would always say that my first pitch in the big leagues was going to be in honor of my father. My dad was a late season call-up in September, but he blew out his elbow so he never got to pitch. He was there to see Stan Musial get his three thousandth career hit, but he never had any official playing time in the big leagues. That pitch was going to be for him. I think that pitch and the opportunity I had to take a picture with him before the game on the field in that ballpark made it a special moment for him.

"What has been fun for me," he continued, "is that the two of us have played in the same ballpark but years apart. Back in 1997, I played in Clinton, Iowa, and an older woman came up to me and said she saw my dad pitch on that same field when she was a thirteen-year-old and now she was here to watch me pitch. It was very cool. Sometimes you think of your parents as old and then you run into this situation and it helps connect the two of you."

◆ JORGE POSADA ◆

Play Ball is a children's book written by Jorge Posada, which tells the story of his childhood and the struggles he endured to become a major leaguer. Posada, who has played for the New York Yankees his entire sixteen-plus-year major-league career, explained, "The book talks about how I grew up and how my father was such an important part of my life."

Posada grew up in Puerto Rico and his hardworking father impacted his life in many ways. "He was my coach every year . . . and he's still my coach," said a grinning Posada. "He knows me better than anyone else. He raised me in the game and we talk all the time. He is a positive influence every time he is around," he added proudly.

The greatest lesson the All-Star catcher learned from his father can be summarized in two words: hard work. "My father at times had four and five jobs to support us and provide us with everything we had," Posada said, "and he still found the time to coach us or go to the playground and play ball."

Posada was selected by the Yankees in the 24th round of the June 1990 draft out of Calhoun Community College in Decatur, Alabama. He made his major-league debut on September 4, 1995, against the Seattle Mariners in Yankee Stadium and his father was there. "It was quite emotional for him and me," recalled Posada. "He still remembers how he cried the first time he saw me out on the field. Even today I always know where my dad is in the ballpark. There might be sixty thousand fans in the stadium, but you know where mom and dad are sitting. Even on the road, when he goes to those games, I've got to find him and see where he is sitting."

It is easy to predict who Posada most admired when he was growing up. "My dad and my mom, they did a lot for me and my sister to help make us who we are."

Prior to the start of the 2012 season, Posada announced his retirement after seventeen years of Major League Baseball all for one team . . . the New York Yankees. In his career, Posada posted a .275 batting average, hit 275 home runs with 1065 RBIS, and was a five time All-Star team selection.

◆ COLBY RASMUS ◆

Baseball Hall of Famer Lefty Gomez once said, "I'd rather be lucky than good." Colby Rasmus has been lucky and good, gaining success on every level in his baseball life.

He was lucky that his father, Tony, a 10th-round selection in 1986 for the California Angels, was a talented and knowledgeable baseball enthusiast who was able to coach Colby during the majority of his life.

"My earliest memory was during coach-pitch ball," Rasmus recalled. "But my greatest memory was playing in the Little League World Series."

Rasmus pitched and played first base for Phenix City, Alabama, in the 1999 Little League World Series in Williamsport, Pennsylvania—home of Little League baseball. His team became the United States Champions, but lost in the finals to a team from Hirakata, Japan.

However, his luck did not end there. Rasmus went to Russell County High School in Seales, Alabama. In 2001, the school got a new baseball coach, Rasmus's father, Tony, who took over a losing baseball program and turned it into a hugely successful one. By the time Colby was a senior in 2005, he was helping to lead his team to the national championship with a .484 average, 24 home runs, and 66 RBI in just 39 games.

That wasn't the only good thing to happen to the young outfielder in 2005. . . . Rasmus followed in his father's footsteps and was selected in the Major League Baseball draft. The St. Louis Cardinals made Colby Rasmus their first-round pick (28th overall) of the June draft. (One year later, Colby's brother, Cory, a right-handed pitcher, kept up the family tradition by getting selected by the Atlanta Braves in the first round.)

The six foot two athlete was named as the Cardinals' top prospect in 2007, 2008, and 2009 by *Baseball America*. On April 7, 2009, Rasmus's luck continued as he made his major-league debut against the Pittsburgh Pirates. Starting in right field, he went two for four in his debut and scored twice.

A man of few words, Colby Rasmus said he owes it all to his father. "I learned everything from my dad," said Rasmus with sincerity. "I was always right under his wing learning everything I could."

◆ JUAN RINCON ◆

Like kids in the United States, Juan Rincon would get up to play baseball on the weekends. However, in Maracaibo, Zulia, Venezuela, where Rincon grew up, field options are very limited. "I remember getting up very early every Sunday and going to the field," he recalled. "It was very early, but that's what happens when you have to share the field with as many teams as there were.

"I remember sitting at the front door of my house, having my breakfast, and getting ready to go to the fields. My father used to wake up each Sunday and ask me if I wanted to go. He used to say, 'Son, you know it's really early, do you want to go to the field today?' I never said no . . . never once, not once did I ever say 'No.' But he would always ask me, 'Do you want to go?' He never forced me to get up, not like school, for which he would say, 'Get up! You gotta get up and get to school.'"

The right-handed pitcher credits his father for his success. "My father was my coach and he did everything for me," said Rincon. "He also would buy a lot of videos and books about the big leagues. He used to teach me, especially about hitting. I wasn't that good at it though," he added with a smile.

"He taught me a lot. He used to take me every afternoon to a field that was close by and hit ground balls to me. Then, as I got older, he used to catch me in the bullpen until I got to be about sixteen years old. After that I got too powerful and threw too hard for him to still be able to catch my pitches. When I was older it was my dad who would take me to the park to run and do drills on the field," recalled the MLB reliever.

"I am a baseball player," Rincon continued, "and was able to play this game for so long because of him. I love this game because of him. In South America we don't always have a lot of things available to people here in the United States. You don't have the same type of system for playing the game as you do here. Your father is the one who takes you to the stadium, to Little League, to games, to practice after the game, to everything."

Rincon was signed by the Minnesota Twins as an amateur free agent in 1996. He rose through the minor leagues and finally made the jump to the majors on June 7, 2001, debuting that night against the Cleveland Indians, with a scoreless inning in relief.

"When I got called up to the big leagues I called my father," he shared, "but I could not talk to him because he was crying. He was in tears. He could not say a word. He then handed the phone to my mother to talk. She thought originally that I was promoted from Double-A to Triple-A but then when I told her what really happened and that I got promoted all the way up to the big leagues, and then she couldn't take it anymore and she had to hand the phone over to my sister. It was very emotional!"

Rincon pitched in just four games in 2001. He got a little more playing time the next season as his career began to take off. "My dad was there in 2002, to see me play at the end of the season in Minnesota. He was very proud," said a humble Rincon.

Rincon said a particular piece of advice from his father remains with him. "Never give up! If you have a goal in your heart you should never give it up. My father taught me that and I will never forget it."

◆ MARIANO RIVERA ◆

Back in the early 1980s, no one would have given Mariano Rivera a second look, not to mention much of a chance of making the major leagues. The Panamanian was just like every other kid in his Puerto Caimito neighborhood, playing soccer or baseball in his free time with makeshift equipment. He didn't have a leather baseball glove until he was twelve years old, when his father, Mariano Sr., bought one for him.

"I learned everything I know from my father," stated Rivera. "My father always told me to work hard. And, whatever you want in life, work hard and you can achieve it."

It is well-documented that Rivera worked three years as a fisherman. Like his father and uncle, he spent six days a week on a boat, filling it with sardines before heading into dock. "It wasn't an easy job. It was hard," Rivera recalled. "Fishing is a hard job. Fishing at night . . . rain . . . day, night," explained Rivera. "You have to be wise and smart . . . and quick. You can't fall asleep on those (boats) because you will get in an accident."

Rivera said the hardships of fishing helped guide him to his true path in life. "I knew that wasn't for me," said Rivera. "I didn't want to be depending on the water, or being a fisherman. It's hard. Extremely hard. I wanted to study to be a mechanic. Obviously I didn't do it, because the Lord had different plans for me."

Those plans, as it turned out, were to become one of the best closers in Major League Baseball history. But that didn't happen overnight.

In 1988, Rivera played shortstop for Panama Oeste, an amateur team representing his area. With his strong defense but weak offense, he was not viewed as a potential major leaguer. The following year, his team's pitcher was performing so badly that Rivera volunteered to pitch. He excelled on the mound— enough to get invited to a Yankees' tryout camp and then get signed by the New York club to a professional contract on February 17, 1990.

The six foot two right-hander didn't know any English, but continued to follow his father's advice and worked hard to learn the language and improve his game. "I don't think I can remember ever having to bring Mariano into the office to have a talk or give advice," said Bill Evers, manager of the Yankees' Triple-A club, the Columbus Clippers. "Mariano always took care of himself. He came with one purpose each day—to get better."

Rivera got the call to the big leagues in May 1995. "It was like, late night," recalled Rivera. "Evers said they called me up. I said, 'What? You're kidding.' Man I was jumping on that bed. I called everybody—my wife (Clara), my parents, my agent. It was," remembered Rivera, "wonderful."

The twelve-time All-Star and five-time world champion is known for his calm demeanor and one pitch—a cut fastball, or "cutter." While Rivera is willing to teach the pitch to anyone, his advice to Little Leaguers is to not even try it. "Don't throw anything else but the fastball," said Rivera. "There is a lot of risk if you try to throw any other pitch. That is what I always threw. Throw the heat, and then when you get bigger and stronger— say when you are fifteen, sixteen, or seventeen years old—then you manipulate pitches. But for right now, when you are younger, throw the fastball as much as possible. That is the best advice I can give Little Leaguers."

◆ RYAN ROBERTS ◆

"My dad was actually my coach all through Little League and up to my high school years," recalled Texas native Ryan Roberts. "He also coached me on my All-Star teams. I remember when I reached high school, he still came around to help the coaches there throw batting practice and he did all he could until I got drafted."

Looking back at his early baseball career, Roberts shared his favorite moment. "I have a video of the first home run I ever hit in Little League. It still makes the *SportsCenter* highlight at the Roberts's household even to this day," Roberts said with a laugh. "My parents still love watching it.

"It's nice seeing how my mom and dad have reacted over the years to my play and I know they are happy that I've made it to the big leagues, knowing the tremendous sacrifices and time they invested in me playing this game I love. And they still spend a lot of time watching and listening to all of the games. For me, it is great to know that I have someone there all the time who is willing to help out and to provide whatever they can. They've done a lot that has gone unnoticed."

Roberts graduated from L.D. Bell High School and went on to Eastfield Junior College in Texas. After his sophomore year, he transferred to the University of Texas at Arlington. His father's advice helped him along the way. "My dad taught me to stay strong in the game," said Roberts. "Baseball is such an emotional game at times. You can go through times when you are at the top of the world, and then in a moment, you're hitting rock bottom. It's hard to go through it if you don't have someone to turn to—if you are by yourself. You have your teammates, but nothing is better than having your family there for encouragement and helping you to remember the good times and letting you know you are there for a reason."

The gregarious infielder said his father also showed him the value of perseverance. "My dad is big on never giving up or quitting," said Roberts. "He doesn't like to quit. If you were slumping or struggling, you can't blame anyone else, you've got to fight through it.

"He was great on teaching me to stay with things and staying strong. You can break down in this game because of the emotional strain it can place on you, so that is why it is important to stay strong. He would say, 'Baseball is a game of failures, if you get three hits out of every ten at-bats then you are having a great season.' I quickly realized with my dad that you can't be perfect in this game. The lessons he taught me have not only prepared me well in baseball, but have helped me grow up as a man."

The Toronto Blue Jays selected Roberts in the 18th round of the June 2003 draft. "I can remember the first game my parents attended when I hit the Short-A season," recalled Roberts of his early days in the New York–Penn League. "It was up in Auburn and the stadium experienced a blackout. So they saw me have one at-bat, and then the lights went out. Fortunately, they've seen me play after that!"

His ability to play many infield positions increased Roberts's value and helped him make it to the majors with the Blue Jays in 2006. Since then he has played for the Texas Rangers and Arizona Diamondbacks—and his father is still there with advice. "Basically, he is still my coach, helping out whenever and wherever he can," explained Roberts. "Of course, the coaches we have here in the organization know a little more about the game," he added with a grin, "but it's still nice hearing from your dad. And, even when he doesn't know it all, it is still good to hear his encouragement."

If it weren't for some timely and sage advice from his father, lefty Nate Robertson would never have stepped across the white lines of a baseball diamond, much less onto a major-league field.

"It was my first baseball memory and probably my worst memory overall," confessed Robertson. "I actually went out for catcher in my first year of organized baseball. I was just five years old. They decided to let kids try out different positions and see what they liked. I'm left-handed, but I threw on some catcher's gear anyway and set up to catch. I then missed the first pitch from the coach and took it right in the chest. I didn't like baseball after that and I really wanted to quit. I developed a fear of the ball, but my dad told me to 'Give it one more chance, and then if you don't like it, you can give it up.'"

Robertson says he doesn't know where his path in life would have led if he hadn't given it one more chance, but stated emphatically, "I am just thankful he encouraged me to give it one more try . . . that's all I can say."

Robertson is not convinced that his father's message would have had as much impact coming from someone else. "Maybe it was the way he said it. The presentation of the message is sometimes more important than the message itself. Meaning, anybody can tell you, 'don't give up,' but coming from my dad, the message was a little deeper than that."

As it turned out, Robertson's father began coaching his sons in the sport they all grew up loving. "Basically, when we got involved with baseball—me and my brothers—my dad was getting involved as well. We all kind of learned the game together that way. As he learned, we learned with him, and he coached us along the way."

Robertson and his brothers continued to receive good advice and life lessons from their father, the coach. "We listened to him, and more than anything—the game aside—it was the discipline that he taught, the character building, and the sense of hard work, which went a lot further than any Little League game.

"He always taught us to 'Go out there and do your very best with what God has given you the ability to do. Try to keep it all in perspective and don't get caught up too much in the hype.'"

Robertson's talent got him drafted twice before he finally signed with the Florida Marlins in 1999. He made his major-league debut in a start three years later, on September 7, 2002, with the Marlins at Pittsburgh. Needless to say, Robertson's father was in attendance for the big game. "It was fun having him there," the young Robertson remembered. "My dad has this ability to put things into perspective when it comes to what happens in life. And, because of that, I grew up a pretty grounded person. My dad had never gotten caught up or involved with all the glitz and glamour. So when a reporter caught up with him at the game and wanted his thoughts about his son being in the big leagues and pitching in this beautiful ballpark, he just told him, 'I just see it as just another old field and playing the game of baseball,'" Robertson recalled with a big smile. "That is always the way he sees things."

It is obvious that Robertson loves and respects his father. He turns to him for advice to this day. "He is the wisest man I ever met," Robertson stated proudly. "That might be a little biased, but it is still a reflection on how he lives his life for me to say that."

He explained further, "Really more than anything my father was my source. It was all biblical for us. I come from a solid family and my father made sure we followed what was right. He was also a military man, so when you mix those two principles together you could never step out of line, even a little bit. Looking back and through it all, I am so thankful for all that and beyond what I learned from him about the game, I learned how it was to be a man."

A great story from Robertson's youth really demonstrates the presence of his father in his life. The redhead also believes it shows the importance of how you should present a message and how it can make all the difference, "One day my brother and I were looking throughout the house for something to eat and we were complaining that we couldn't find anything," Robertson recalled. "We weren't too happy with our choices of what we found.

"My dad always stressed to us to be content with who you are, what you have, and to be thankful and never be in the state of want or need. So as we were sitting around complaining about the food, my dad overheard us. He told us to go into the other room. He then came out with two plates and an opened can of sauerkraut. He then told us to eat every bit of the sauer-kraut and that was all we were going to get. And then he said that we were going to be happy with the sauerkraut and that he didn't want to hear us ever complain again that there wasn't any food in the house to eat.

"I learned my lesson that day. I can't remember the last time I complained about any food I ate. I'm pretty happy with what I get."

Robertson took that lesson to another level when he was playing in Detroit, where he developed a reputation as one of the really good guys in the game for escorting homeless people to a local diner, located near the stadium, and making sure they received a good meal.

One "food" he definitely doesn't complain about is chewing gum. He was the creator of the wildly popular "Gum Time" rally in Detroit in 2006, when he stuffed as much gum as he could into his mouth as the Tigers mounted a comeback. The Tigers made it all the way to the World Series that season.

That was definitely a high note in his career, but Robertson remains on an even keel concluding, "My dad helped me learn how to go about living my life, which will lead into anything I ever do—whether it's baseball, or any occupation or task I'm involved in."

The gregarious lefty was born in Wichita, Kansas, and stays close to his family and his roots as part owner of the Wichita Wingnuts, an Independent League team his brother helps to run.

◆ SEAN RODRIGUEZ ◆

Sean Rodriguez was destined to be a Major League Baseball player. With all the work his father, Johnny, put into coaching him, what else could he become?

Johnny Rodriguez has spent much of his life playing and coaching baseball. He has scouted for major-league teams, coached for a high school, and a couple of colleges, and coached and managed in the minor leagues. In 2010, he became manager of the Quad City River Bandits of the St. Louis Cardinals organization.

Sean Rodriguez was selected by the Anaheim Angels in the 3rd round of the June 2003 draft. The second baseman made his major-league debut on April 19, 2008, against the Seattle Mariners. Though he was extremely proud of his son for making it to the big leagues, Johnny Rodriguez could not be there for Sean's first major-league game. "He was actually coaching when I made my big-league debut," said Rodriguez. "He was working, but he was listening to the game on the radio."

Rodriguez credits his father for his baseball success. "My dad still throws me batting practice, but he has been coaching me ever since I could pick up a baseball. He was my first coach and will continue to be all my life," stated the six foot infielder.

"I remember when I turned four or five years old he started coaching professionally with the Yankees organization," Rodriguez continued. "Today he is with the Cardinals. He was gone most of the time, but when he was in town he made it a point to coach me. My dad spent a lot of time with me and my brother. I am actually very grateful for it. Some guys might get a little spoiled having their father as their coach, but not me. My dad wasn't like that . . . even though he was never hard on me, never screamed at me, never got mad at me, and never called me out on the field. My dad was great. When I did do something wrong he was more quiet than anything else and then I knew something was wrong. He wouldn't even say anything when I got back to the car. He always wanted me to figure out what I did wrong. I remember when I used to see him obviously down, I'd say to myself, 'What did I do? What did I do?' I would think this to myself. It then got me thinking—what did I do wrong? I would then have to figure it out on my own. That was his biggest thing—for me to figure it out on my own. It was his way of teaching me a lesson—a lesson for me to self-teach myself, self-correct myself, and self-discipline myself."

Rodriguez recalled one of his funniest early baseball memories. "It involved this bat someone gave my dad as a gift when I was in Little League," he shared. "I must have been eleven or twelve years old. My dad wanted me to use the bat, because he wanted to see me swing a big bat. But the bat always sounded a little funny to me and I guess it did to the other team we were playing against this one day. It sounded like a dead bat. Apparently I used to have some good power even though I was little, but the team we were playing against thought I had corked the bat. I kid you not! They paid $200 to have the bat popped off to prove they were right. I remember it was a playoff game and the other team put the game under protest, claiming the bat I was using was corked. I didn't get it at the time. I didn't even have a hit in that game, just two walks. But they said to the umpire that they were playing the game under protest. My mom and brother, who were there, were really concerned. The other team kept putting the bat in their dugout, and my brother kept bringing it back to ours.

"I said to the other team and the umpire that 'You can't pop the bat unless you pay me for it.' I think back now and laugh—it's Little League and they were making this big deal about it! I knew it wasn't corked, so eventually they paid me the $200 and I gave them the bat. Once they got it, everything stopped—our game and the games on the other fields. Everything stopped! Then someone from the other team ran over to the concession stand and grabbed a hammer and a screwdriver. They popped off the top and nothing came out. I knew it. Well, then the other team's coach came over to me and apologized and then said kiddingly, 'I do have to ask, can we check your arm, and how much would it cost to check that?'"

Rodriguez obviously has talent and some of the fastest feet in the big leagues when turning a double play. In his, thus far, brief major-league career, he has gotten better each season. With his father still active in baseball, it's not surprising that Rodriguez still turns to him for advice. "How do I not?" he asked. "He is older than I and he has all those years of experience. Why wouldn't I ask him for advice? He has worked with so many superstars over the years. How could I not think of asking him?" said the Miami, Florida, native.

"But that is the thing about my dad. When I do ask him a question or questions he'll always say, 'Well, think about it! Come back to me with an answer and I'll let you know if you're right and until then I'm not giving you the answer.'

"It's like Little League all over again. He never gives in. Sometimes it gets frustrating. I'll think to myself, 'Come on, just give me the answer!' But he'll say, 'No.' He always wants me to think about it. He tells me that I'll be thankful when I'm older. My dad always tells me that I am going to be my own best hitting coach. He says, 'I'm not always going to be there, I can be your second-best hitting coach, but you need to be your first-best hitting coach.'"

Rodriguez wanted to pass on some of his own advice to Little Leaguers. "It's all about hard work," Rodriguez stated. "Ask yourself, 'Did I truly work hard today? And, did I truly outwork everyone else today?' Remember the minute you sit down is the moment that the guy next to you is taking your job because he was the one outworking you. So keep asking yourself, 'Did I truly outwork the guy next to me and did I push myself to be the best?'"

◆ KENNY ROGERS ◆

Sometimes, the most unlikely situations make the best success stories, as is the case with Kenny Rogers.

Rogers played Little League baseball like many other kids. His dad was his coach for a couple of seasons. But with his father in the Air Force, the Rogers family traveled quite a bit. Many of the young Rogers's Little League games were played on different Air Force bases. When his father retired, they settled in Plant City, Florida, and became strawberry farmers.

"Plant City is home to the best strawberries in the world!" claimed Rogers. "But picking them takes a lot of work."

Tending the strawberries took . . . so much work that he was not even able to play baseball in high school until his senior year. But strawberries were also the inspiration for the best advice he received from his father.

"One of the greatest lessons my dad taught me was picking strawberries. . . . If you ever picked strawberries, it's not like picking an apple or an orange, you know how much work is involved," Rogers explained. "My dad taught me the concept of hard work. Unfortunately, I was never that good at picking strawberries, not because I didn't like hard work, but I just never had the knack for it. And because of all the work we had to do to keep up the farm, I couldn't devote all the time I wanted to baseball, especially when I got to high school. I wasn't able to play until my senior year.

"But I was very fortunate," he added. "I had good people around me and because of the small size of our town at that time, the support everyone gave me and my family was tremendous."

That support led to good things. At the age of seventeen, Rogers was drafted by the Texas Rangers in the 39th round in June 1982. The left-hander played for years in the minors before finally making it to the majors in 1989. "My parents came to my first major-league game," recalled Rogers, of his April 6, 1989, debut with the Rangers. "But I remember them more so traveling and seeing me in the minor leagues. I spent seven years in the minors and my family was always there for me. They helped me financially back then whenever they could. They couldn't always give much, but whatever they had they were there for me.

It helped me to try even harder and it made me more dedicated because of the sacrifices they made on my behalf."

Thinking back, Rogers was reminded of another lesson learned from his father. "I was a kid that got in trouble a lot and I always enjoyed baseball. I remember my dad telling me one day I wasn't going to play for a week or two. I forgot what I did wrong," chuckled the four-time All-Star. "But it must have been pretty bad. He knew I loved baseball more than anything. So when he told me that, it really hurt me because I lived for playing baseball. I also remember the big game was coming up and I asked him again if I was going to play. 'No way,' he said. 'You are still being punished,' he told me. So I walked back to my room disappointed. Then an hour or so before the game, I saw him carry my equipment to the car, but he never let on why he did it. My dad then came to my room and said, 'You're going to the game, but you're sitting in the stands to watch the game and you're not playing.' I thought to myself this was even worse. It was like double punishment. This was murder.

"When we got to the stadium, I went to the stands to sit. My dad told me that I had a responsibility to my team and to myself. He then told me that he was going to let me play. It was a lesson I will never forget."

The twenty-year MLB veteran and five-time Gold Glove winner also got his best baseball advice from his father. "I think for me in baseball I try to do the best, not just for myself, but for my teammates, because I know they are relying on me and I have a responsibility to them. My dad helped me learn that early on," explained Rogers. "I have a job to do not just for myself, but for the people who have faith in me. You don't just go out there and do things without thinking of your team because of the tremendous faith they have for you.

"It's easy to go out and play when you feel good and everything is great. You usually find out what you are made of when you go out there when you feel terrible or from a pitching standpoint you have a bad outing. When you really feel like there is not much of a chance to be successful and you still go out there anyway. I actually feel more pride and satisfaction in going out there and getting the victory when I'm not at my best. I appreciate it when I see it in other teammates and hopefully

they see it in me and feel the same way. You want your teammates to go out and compete no matter what the odds are
against them."

So the boy who loved baseball, but had little opportunity to
play in high school, ended up having a very impressive major-
league career. "I never really had any idols or heroes growing up.
I never thought about playing baseball professionally," Rogers
recalled. "My parents wanted me to be successful, but they also
wanted me to be happy. I have two boys of my own and they
want to do what I did and one day they want to follow in my
footsteps. For me there have been a lot of rewards playing this
game, but you do miss a lot of time with your kids being gone so
much. This is a tough career and it's not worth it sometimes
being away as much as you are. My family means everything to
me."

Rogers's father, Ed, remains a big part of his family life. "I
still talk to my dad all the time," he said fondly. "And it's not so
much about how to hit or how to throw or about baseball technique anymore. It's just talk, father and son."

◆ SCOTT ROLEN ◆

Scott Rolen is a Rookie of the Year Award winner, a world champion, a seven-time All-Star and the winner of eight Gold Gloves. But the most important thing to him always has been—and always will be—his family. It is a priority that was instilled in him at an early age by his parents.

"My dad was my head coach in Little League," said Rolen. "He enjoyed being out there as much as we did. My dad did everything he had to do for us. He was first a dad out there and he certainly didn't push me into playing," he noted.

"I remember it wasn't about competition," Rolen continued. "It wasn't a 'dog eat dog,' or try to get better, or even have a career thing. I was there to have fun. It was the main thing . . . something I hope isn't lost on a lot of kids these days."

Rolen recalled his youth with fondness. "I played a lot of baseball in my life. The thing I can remember most was the anticipation of going to play on Saturday morning. Whether it was T-ball or Pee Wee Baseball, I couldn't wait until Saturday and how much fun it was going to be."

The big third baseman was selected out of high school in the 2nd round of the June 1993 draft by the Philadelphia Phillies. He made his major-league debut on August 1, 1996. He was hit by a pitch that ended his first season after just 130 at-bats, allowing him to be eligible for Rookie of the Year consideration in 1997.

Rolen, who grew up in Jasper, Indiana, was traded in 2002 to St. Louis, where he became a National League champion in 2004 and a world champion in 2006. He was traded to Toronto in 2008 and then the following year to Cincinnati, where his veteran leadership helped the Reds win their division in 2009. He has fought through injuries and has been an All-Star seven times. And his parents have seen it all. They attend as many games as they can, which wouldn't be so unusual except that Rolen's mother is afraid to fly, so they drive everywhere to catch their youngest son in action.

Rolen recalled the first major-league game they attended. "It was my first game ever in Philadelphia," he said. "My parents literally drove all night to be there for the game. To this day, I would say that it was my most emotional moment in baseball. I remember my parents got to the stadium in the fourth inning. I saw them walking down to their seats and I was in the field. It was tough to put into words how I felt during that moment. I've played in the World Series and in All-Star Games, but seeing my parents walk to their seats during my first game was the best baseball moment ever."

Rolen now has a family of his own and tries to instill in his two children the same values his father instilled in him. "The greatest lesson my dad taught me had nothing to do with baseball. He taught us, or tried to teach us, to be respectful of others, try to be a good person, and treat people well. To him it is more important what you do off the field than on the field," said Rolen. "Whether we played baseball, basketball, football, or whatever we did, he was always there to support us. He loved us and that was the main thing. I grew up in a loving family."

◆ JIMMY ROLLINS ◆

Jimmy Rollins grew up in Oakland, California, playing baseball all day and watching his favorite player, Rickey Henderson, all night.

"My dad was my coach. He was my dad when we were off the field . . . and when we were on the field, he still did everything he could for me," said Rollins.

Both of his parents were strong influences in his life—particularly his early life, according to Rollins. "My dad probably taught me about determination more than anything. Baseball came easy to me. I have been playing the game since I was four and it has always been my passion," the speedy shortstop shared.

Rollins was selected by the Philadelphia Phillies in the 2nd round of the June 1996 draft out of Encinal High School. He made his major-league debut on September 17, 2000, against the Florida Marlins. He walked in his first plate appearance and later tripled for his first major-league hit. From that point on, his career took off. Rollins has been the National League MVP, a World Series champion, and a three-time All-Star.

"Both my parents are very proud," said the likable Rollins with a big grin. "Every time I go home, my mom gets the chance to tell everyone about her son, the major-league ballplayer!"

He still talks regularly to both his parents, but "concerning baseball not as much anymore," he explained. "We do talk about whether I had a good game or how things are going. I talk to my mom a lot about the game because she used to play softball pretty seriously."

Thinking back on his career to this point, Rollins knows how lucky he has been. "It was my dream and I was able to fulfill that dream. I also know it is a lot of kids' dream out there," he said reflectively. "I am very fortunate to play and compete at this level."

◆ JUSTIN RUGGIANO ◆

Justin Ruggiano and his younger brother, Brian, grew up in Austin, Texas. "Our father coached us mostly in Little League from T-ball, through coach-pitch, and all the way through kid-pitch," said the elder brother.

"He was my main coach and he pretty much taught me all the ins and outs of the game," said Ruggiano. "He was always willing to work with me whenever I needed him—whether it was on a Saturday afternoon and he was hitting me ground balls, throwing batting practice to me, or catching me whenever I pitched."

Ruggiano went on to Blinn Junior College, before transferring to Texas A&M University.

"My father really taught me how to be competitive," said the six foot two athlete. "He taught me how to win. That was a pretty good lesson if you think about it. And that works in baseball as well as in life."

In 2004, the Los Angeles Dodgers selected Ruggiano in the 25th round of the June draft. He was traded to the Tampa Bay Devil Rays in July 2006. The trade gave him the opportunity to make it to the majors on September 19, 2007.

Ruggiano's brother followed in his footsteps. Brian went to Texas A&M (although as a catcher), and he was also selected by the Dodgers in the 25th round in the June 2008 draft. Justin said the brothers also mimic one another with their performances on particular days. "For example, he'll hit a home run one night and so will I, or he'll hit a double and a couple of singles and go three for four and so will I.

"It's really strange and yet it's pretty cool. Even though we are four years apart and it's not a twin thing, it does happen a lot."

Ruggiano said his father also remains connected to him in ways that seem difficult to explain. "My dad has these premonitions," Ruggiano shared. "He'll often say that I'll do this or that during a game—and it generally happens."

Ruggiano's career has had its ups and downs, but through it all, his father has been there for him. "I reach out to my dad multiple times a week and I talk with him," said Ruggiano. "We talk all of the time and I ask him advice as much as I can. He is older and wiser than me. He's lived a good and productive life, so it only makes sense for me to go to him for advice."

◆ B. J. RYAN ◆

"The best part of being a major-league player is that you play a kid's game and you still get to have fun with it," admitted Robert Victor (B. J.) Ryan. "The camaraderie in the clubhouse and the friends you make and just being able to go out each day and compete day in and day out . . . this is the best part for me about being a major leaguer."

Ryan played the "kid's game" when he was a kid as well, and he was coached by his father for a few of those Little League years. "Growing up, I will admit that my dad was a little tougher on me," said the six foot five lefty, "but he always wanted me to do the best. He did it because he wanted me to be successful and these were the lessons I was able to learn at a very young age."

Ryan pitched in the majors for ten seasons, making his major-league debut with his only appearance with the Cincinnati Reds on July 28, 1999, and then pitched over six seasons with the Baltimore Orioles and four with the Toronto Blue Jays.

He still talks to his father. "Today, it's about a lot of normal stuff. He's always been a great dad and he was a great coach," said the Louisiana native. "You learn your lessons growing up; you learn your failures and accept it. My father is always there if I need to talk."

◆ CURT SCHILLING ◆

Some fathers and sons have such a strong bond that a relationship of sorts continues even after one is gone. This is the case with Curt Schilling and his father.

It has been well documented that Curt Schilling continued to leave a ticket for his father for every game he pitched even after he died in 1988. "Before he passed away my dad never missed a game," the big right-hander explained. "It is a tribute to him. I'm raising four kids and he wasn't around to see them, so there is a legacy there I am passing on to them. I hope one day my kids will look at me the way I used to look at my dad. That's my goal."

From the very beginning, baseball was an important part of Schilling's life, thanks to his dad. "I remember my mom telling me the day I came home from the hospital my dad had a ball and glove in my chair," Schilling recalled. "He was always a baseball fan."

Schilling's father coached him throughout his Little League career and was ecstatic when he was selected in the 2nd round of the January 1986 draft (the last January draft in Major League Baseball history) by the Boston Red Sox.

"My dad and I were very, very close until he passed away in 1988," Schilling recalled fondly. "I was twenty one. His biggest desire for me was effort. He didn't care how good I was at anything as long as I did everything the best I could do it. He coached with that attitude. I always wanted to win, but that was never the priority. The priority was playing the game right and playing the game hard."

Schilling's effort showed though his stellar twenty-year MLB league career, which started in 1988 with the Baltimore Orioles. The six-time All-Star also played for the Houston Astros, Philadelphia Phillies, Arizona Diamondbacks, and Boston Red Sox. He pitched in the World Series in 1993 with the Phillies and became a world champion with the Diamondbacks in 2001, then again with the Red Sox in 2004 and 2007.

His father wasn't physically around for his major-league career, but his perspective on being a major leaguer stayed with Schilling. "My father considered some things more important on the field and some things more important off the field," he said. "I played this game for the respect of the players I played with and against. And off the field, you have a tremendous window as a major leaguer to support whatever cause that you choose. So you have to take advantage of those situations."

Schilling and his family support several causes, mainly, the Amyotrophic Lateral Sclerosis Association (which is dedicated to fighting what is commonly known as Lou Gehrig's disease), the Shade Foundation (an organization dedicated to eradicating melanoma through education, detection, and prevention of skin cancer), and the Asperger's Association of New England. The people who benefit from this support are deeply grateful, but his father would be the one who is most proud of the man Schilling has become.

♦ MIKE SCIOSCIA ♦

Even those that teach and coach now had to start somewhere. Mike Scioscia, manager of the Los Angeles Angels of Anaheim began learning the game from his father.

"My dad worked a lot, but he loved baseball and some of my earliest memories are playing baseball with my dad in my backyard. It was a great experience. My dad and I were very close and he helped me learn a lot about the game and about life," recalled Scioscia.

"My dad was always my coach in Little League up until I was about thirteen years old," he continued. "He was always supportive. My dad instilled a level of confidence in me. I always felt that I could do this and that, and that I am doing it right, and to keep playing. I remember whenever we'd play, he'd say supportive things like, 'Hey that was good!'

"My dad had a love of the game. He never was professionally trained, but he always enjoyed the game and he knew I did, too. As he coached me he passed on what he picked up and learned about the game. To me that was the best teacher experience anyway."

Scioscia grew up outside of Philadelphia and went to Springfield (Delaware County) High School. He passed on a scholarship to Clemson University when the Los Angeles Dodgers selected him with their first pick of the June 1976 draft (19th overall selection).

Scioscia made his major-league debut on April 20, 1980 and the catcher, known for his defense, became a two-time All-Star in over twelve seasons with the Dodgers.

He started a very successful managerial career with the Angels in 2000, guiding the club to their first World Championship in 2002 and twice earning American League Manager of the Year honors.

Scioscia is married with a son and daughter. "My dad passed away quite a few years ago," he said. "But over the years I have always thought of him. Now that I am a dad there are a lot of things that I can relate to."

He continued, "My dad got the opportunity to watch me play along the way when I hit the minors. He didn't see my first game in the major leagues, but he did get to see me a few games later. We played a series in Philadelphia and he was there. Through the years, my dad would always let me know how proud he was of me.

"I thought of my dad a lot during the World Series in 2002. Now that I am in the process of raising my own children, I often think of my parents. I think you find yourself turning into your parents."

◆ CHRIS SHELTON ◆

Chris Shelton's father coached him from Little League all the way through high school in his native Utah.

"The biggest lesson I learned from my dad was to always play hard and have fun," said Shelton. "When I was in Little League he told me not to take the game too seriously, especially at that level. He'd say that it's all about fun, it's just a game and that is what it is all about. He'd say, 'Have fun with your buddies.' My dad was always out there and I think he had as much fun on the field as I did," recalled the redhead.

"My dad always had a lot of joy in seeing me play and he still does today and it's great having him there."

Although Shelton's first baseball memory does not specifically involve his father, it does revolve around the joy of playing the game that his father instilled in him. "For me, my first memory was going out there and playing that first Little League game," Shelton recalled. "I couldn't tell you when it was . . . some Saturday a long time ago. Putting that uniform on for the first time and getting dirty—that was the biggest thing for me."

The first baseman still talks to his father frequently. "I call him every day," Shelton said. "After each game I call him and we talk. Sometimes it's the same conversation, but we still talk and it's always fun."

Shelton said talking to his father is as informative and helpful as it is enjoyable. "He always talks about the confidence he has for me and knowing that he is always there supporting me is really a nice thing," Shelton admitted. "When I have questions, he is definitely one of the first people I go to."

◆ JAMES SHIELDS ◆

James Shields has been pitching in the majors since 2006. His road to the majors started when he was very young, with his father by his side. "He coached me a few years or so in Little League, but my dad was more a coach for me off the field—practicing at home and working on things and helping me to stay committed," said Shields. "He coached my older brothers, too, on some of their teams, but he liked to do that private instruction as much as possible at home and off the field. My dad never wanted to show favoritism, so I think that is why he felt more comfortable doing what he did off the field . . . and with two older brothers, he was constantly playing with us."

But Shields found out that his father had his limits. "When I was eleven or twelve years old, I asked my dad if he could catch me because I needed to throw a little bullpen session. It was also at the point when I could throw a little harder," said the right-hander. "He agreed to catch me and then I threw one that caught him pretty hard on the leg. I think that was the last time he ever caught me. He said, 'You are throwing a little too hard for your father.' Fortunately, he could pawn me off to my two older brothers."

Shields said the greatest lesson he learned from his father, the coach, was the importance of perseverance. "When you start something, you always have to finish it—no matter whether it's a good job or not a good job," said Shields, recalling his father's advice. "Either way, at the end of the day, you've got to finish the job."

The California native said his parents' contribution to his development as a player and as a person went well beyond imparting a single lesson. "My dad did a lot of things for me," Shields said, growing contemplative. "I think the thing that stands out for me—and what I am most proud of—was all the time, traveling, and money they spent to get me here and there so I could follow my dream. You never realize when you are young how much they really do for you. Looking back, they did a ton for me and my brothers—and especially for me to get to the big leagues. It must be pretty gratifying for them. I know they are smiling."

Shields went to William S. Hart High School in California. As a junior, he was named the *Los Angeles Times* Valley Player of the Year in 1999. The following year he was selected by the Tampa Bay Devil Rays in the 16th round of the June draft.

His quest to reach the majors came to fruition on May 31, 2006, with a start against the Baltimore Orioles. "My parents flew out to Baltimore and they were there for me for my first game," Shields recalled. "It was pretty special for them to see how far I've come as a ballplayer, and where I am now is pretty special for them as well," said Shields, who gained his first All-Star Game selection in 2011.

His father still plays an important role in his life. "I always talk to my dad and turn to him for advice . . . especially if I need advice about my house or my car or something like that," Shields revealed with a laugh. "I am constantly calling him, asking him, 'How do I fix this?' or 'How do I fix that?' and then he gives me a hard time about baseball. He'll tell me how bad I did that day and then he jokes about it with me. He always keeps me in check as much as he can. My dad keeps me grounded. When you do something wrong, you know your dad is always watching."

◆ KELLY SHOPPACH ◆

"From an early age, I had a plan," stated Kelly Shoppach. "When I turned eight years old I wanted to be a professional baseball player. I know a lot of people said that was early to start thinking about it, but from that point on my dad did everything he could to get me there and for me to achieve my dream, including going to college."

Shoppach said his father coached him in Little League until he was twelve or thirteen years old and remained a trusted adviser after that. "I remember it was my dad that really encouraged me to go to college instead of going right to pro ball," said Shoppach. "He also knew that if I didn't have what it takes to play this game, I would have something to fall back on."

After graduating from Brewer High School in Fort Worth, Texas, Shoppach went to Baylor University, where he received the Johnny Bench Award as the nation's top collegiate catcher in his junior year, 2001.

Shoppach was selected by the Boston Red Sox in the 2nd round of the June 2001 draft. He made his debut with the Red Sox on May 28, 2005, at Yankee Stadium. "My first major-league game was on my father's birthday," said Shoppach. "I made my major-league debut on his special day, and it was the best birthday present he ever got. You can bet on that!"

The father and son remain in touch. "Today we bounce ideas off each other all of the time and we see who has the best plan," said Shoppach. "He will always be my dad and, for the most part, I will always take his advice . . . probably blindly using it at times. Even when I got involved in pro ball, we still would talk about hitting and he has always been a factor in my life. My dad has always been a good mental coach for me and not just with sports, but with everything. Once I did get to a level where I knew more than he did, he knew he had to let the baseball coaching go."

But the advice Shoppach received from his father when he was growing up still rings true to this day. "My dad always stressed hustle and effort," recalled Shoppach. "He would say, 'Hustle and effort never go into a slump. Your hitting and defense will come and go, but your ability to hustle and your effort is something you will control all of the time.'"

♦ MATT STAIRS ♦

Matt Stairs played a lot of ice hockey and baseball when he was a kid. But since he is Canadian, one might assume hockey would have won out . . . not in his case.

"Back in Canada it was called the Beaver Leagues," Stairs explained about his early baseball career. "The team I played for was the Miners and my dad was my coach. I always played pitcher or shortstop back then. It was kind of nice having him as my coach. I never had to worry about being late for a game," he added with a wry grin.

"I remember I hit a home run when I played for the Miners," recalled Stairs. "I hit it out of the stadium and it landed in the river. Back then, when I was twelve years old, I wish it would have been on *SportsCenter*. And that was the first and best memory I have growing up," he stated proudly.

A major leaguer now for nearly two decades, Stairs had his parents' support all through his childhood, no matter what sport he chose. "My dad never pushed me to play baseball . . . maybe because I played so much hockey. In baseball, he always told me to be myself and to have fun. My dad never, ever put any pressure on me to play," the outfielder emphatically stated. "I do remember playing from the moment the sun came up until the sun went down. I played baseball all day during the summer and, of course, when winter came, I was playing hockey. My parents through all this were extremely supportive."

The veteran player made his major-league debut on May 29, 1992, with the Montreal Expos and played for thirteen different MLB teams in his career. "My father first saw me play in 1992. I was with Montreal and I ended up hitting a double in that game," Stairs recalled.

Through it all, his father has always been there for Stairs. "My dad is my best friend," said Stairs. "I still call him two or three times a week. It is one of those things. I talk to him and he always says how proud he is of me. We do talk about hitting more so these days, because he knows I'm getting older and I can't get the ball in the air as much as I want to anymore. But my dad still has so much confidence in me. He'll say to me, 'I think you're going to get a home run tonight.' And that's just what I need to hear."

◆ SHANNON STEWART ◆

Shannon Stewart began his training to become a Major League Baseball player at an early age, thanks to his father. "My dad was my coach in Little League," said Stewart. "He was the guy who taught me to play baseball. When I was three or four years old I got my first *Flintstone*-style big old chunky bat and ball. He'd throw the ball and I'd hit it back. Before I played any organized baseball, my dad would have a catch with me and hit ground balls and throw batting practice. He did this for about a year before I got to an organized level. It really made a big difference; I was ready to play before I even got there.

"My dad really prepared me for what was to come. My dad was smart. He also put me on a soccer team thinking that would help me with my coordination. He then worked with me with my baseball. By the time that was all done, he placed me in an organized league and I was ready."

His father taught him to play baseball, but he also imparted some great advice to his blossoming baseball player. "My dad always taught me to be respectful of others," stated Stewart. "He also always told me to learn as much as I can and to ask questions. He'd say, 'Try to further your knowledge in the world.' As for baseball, he helped me develop my passion and drive. He was always encouraging, with words like, 'Do your best!' and 'Always try and succeed.' And, he told me as long as you have that drive to play, you'll be around this game as long as you can."

Stewart graduated from Southridge High School in Miami, Florida. In his senior year, he was selected by the Toronto Blue Jays in the first round (19th overall) of the June 1992 draft and his professional career began.

"I came up with the Blue Jays and my dad came to my very first game in Toronto," the likable outfielder recalled of his MLB playing debut against Detroit on September 8, 1995. "My mom and dad were both there and it was so nice for them to see me play. At that time, when players first got called up, the organization would invite your family into the field to take pictures with you. I remember they were smiling and they were very happy.

"It was a long time ago and I'm glad it was a long time ago, because that means that I've been in this business for awhile. It was a day I will never forget and I am sure they won't either."

Stewart continues to stay in touch with his father. "My father is still—and I believe will always be—involved in my life," Stewart said sincerely. "He helps me to make a lot of my decisions. I sometimes feel like I can't make a decision without him and his advice. He's always been involved in my personal life, my family life, and my baseball life. I will always welcome his advice and, believe it or not, I really do listen to him. And, to his credit, his advice always seems to work out."

◆ MARK SWEENEY ◆

Mark Sweeney played for seven different teams in the majors for thirteen seasons as a first baseman, outfielder, and as a tremendous pinch hitter.

He grew up in Massachusetts, where his dad coached him and his three brothers in Little League. "I was the last of four," explained Sweeney. "It was a good feeling knowing your dad was always there."

Sweeney said his dad was there for him, along with his love for the game, even before he started playing baseball. "What I remember most were the parades we had in our small town to commemorate the start of Little League," shared Sweeney. "I was a batboy first and I wore this shirt that was down to my ankles. I don't even remember wearing my underwear underneath. But I was in the parade holding the sign for our team and my dad, who was the coach, and who was walking behind me and there I was tripping over my shirt. It is what baseball players at this level remember the most—those days when we were kids and going back to those times, knowing how important it was.

"I remember a few years back I was with St. Louis and we were playing San Diego in Hawaii," Sweeney continued. "It was an exhibition series, but it counted. So we all went over there and we had a day off and a bunch of us guys took a tour of the island. We rented a limo bus and we wanted to see the sights. We pulled up to a Little League field. We stepped off the bus and we all got out. The memories for me and the rest of the guys all started to come back to us. We got to see the big, chunky kid, who played catcher, hit a home run over the outfielders' heads, and everyone running around trying to get the ball . . . and the big kid was trucking around the bases as fast as he could—and it wasn't that fast. It is funny because they were the same visions we all had growing up when we were young . . . it all kind of hit home for us.

"That is the fun part of it and that is how you have to keep it," he summarized. "Sometimes at this level it's hard to do, but you have to do it as much as possible because it is still a game and you have to have fun."

Sweeney graduated from Holliston High School and ultimately went to the University of Maine, where he earned a business degree. The California Angels selected him in the 9th round of the June 1991 draft. They traded him to the St. Louis Cardinals on July 8, 1995, and he made his major-league debut shortly thereafter on August 4 against the Chicago Cubs . . . and the rest, as they say, is history.

"Just always be there for your kids. My mom and dad were always there for me," advised Sweeney, who played in the majors for fourteen years.

"I made it a point of remembering my mom and dad with their names on every baseball hat I had. It was the first thing I did once I got a new hat.

It wasn't just my dad who was there all the time; my mom was in the stands cheering us on. It started in Little League and that is what I remember most about them. Whatever sporting event I was in, they made it a point of being there and I think being there for your kids is very, very important. It helps to develop that family bond that goes a long way. So I used to put them on my hat because I want them to always be there. It is a little remembrance of the most important people in my life. I also have the names of my father's two brothers, who passed away, and the great Jimmy Reese, because he was one of those guys I thought I needed to meet in baseball," said Sweeney, referring to the former batboy, New York Yankee, Babe Ruth roommate, scout, coach, and manager who played a part in major-league and minor-league baseball for seventy-eight years. "But it all started with my mom and dad. We are very close."

♦ NICK SWISHER ♦

Being the son of a major leaguer has its advantages: growing up around baseball; learning all the nuances of the game; and, most important, getting the genes of an elite player. Nick Swisher was one of those lucky ones. His father, Steve, was an All-Star catcher for the Chicago Cubs, St. Louis Cardinals, and San Diego Padres who played in the majors from 1974 to 1982, and passed down his DNA and knowledge to his son.

"My dad taught me the importance of hard work. No doubt about it," said major-league outfielder, first baseman, all-star, and all-around nice guy Nick Swisher. "I've always been a hard worker and that is why I'm here—because of that. My dad was a driving force for that and so was my grandma. She was a big influence, too. She helped me out a tremendous amount. I was lucky, though. I kind of grew up in this game and it couldn't be helped. I was three years old when my dad retired from the game. So I guess you can say I've been around this game all my life."

Swisher said his first memory of baseball came when he was six years old. "I got this Wiffle-ball machine. I was so excited and we set it up in the living room right away. I hit a couple of pictures, broke a couple of frames, and that was the last time I hit inside the house," recalled the likable player with a grin.

Like his father, Swisher was a first-round selection in the June draft. The Oakland A's selected him with the 16th overall pick in the 2002 draft out of Ohio State University. He rose quickly through the A's minor-league system and made his major-league debut on September 3, 2004.

"My first game in the big leagues was up in Toronto. I was so excited to get the call-up," said the charismatic Swisher. "My dad drove nine hours from West Virginia and he didn't even tell me that he was coming. And because I didn't know, I didn't even get a chance to leave him tickets for my first game. He had to pay for his own tickets. He certainly surprised me and it was pretty sweet."

Like his father, Swisher added an All-Star appearance to his list of baseball accomplishments, gaining the honor while playing for the New York Yankees. Steve Swisher's All-Star appearance came in 1976 when he played for the Chicago Cubs.

Swisher knows he is lucky to play the game for a living and

shares his good fortune through generous donations to numerous charities and by giving advice to kids. "It's funny, even though I've been able to take my game to a major-league level, I still enjoy watching a Little League game," Swisher explained. "It is sad, though, there seems to be so much pressure on these kids nowadays to win and that is not what the game is all about at that level. When you are in Little League it is about having fun, because you don't want to drive a kid away from the game. The biggest things I tell kids is: have fun; enjoy playing; and if you don't have fun, then don't play."

◆ TAYLOR TANKERSLEY ◆

Thanks to his genes, Taylor Tankersley had some great advantages in life right from the start. With a grandfather (Earl) who played in the St. Louis Browns minor-league system and a father (Tom) who is a nuclear physicist, Tankersley had the makings of a very intelligent baseball player.

He started his road to the majors with his father as his coach. "My dad coached me until I was twelve years old," said the left-handed reliever, "and then he passed the job over to someone who had a little more baseball knowledge. That has always been the best thing about my dad. It wasn't what he knew, but he was really good at understanding what he didn't know."

Tankersley was drafted by the Kansas City Royals in the 39th round of the June draft in his 2001 senior year, but did not sign. He instead went on to the University of Alabama.

"Probably the greatest lesson my dad taught me was his sense of 'stick-to-it-ness' and to always keep a positive attitude," said Tankersley. "He also stressed—and would say—that your attitude is the only thing you yourself can control in this game."

Tankersley stuck with baseball and was selected again, this time in the first round (27th overall) of the June 2004 draft by the Florida Marlins. And so began his professional baseball career.

"My dad taught me that attitude was so important and has always helped me with the mental approach to this game, more so than the technical side of the game," explained Tankersley. "My father is an intelligent man and is smart enough to know he had to give way to the athletic side of the game to those who did what they do best. This game can be a grind and, even to this day, my father can coach me on attitude and the mental aspects of the sport. Baseball can really beat you down at times, but my dad . . . continues to be a driving force in my life. I hope he never stops coaching me at that level."

Tankersley got the call to the majors not long after starting his pro career, making his Major League Baseball debut on June 3, 2006, with the Marlins. "I got called up first when we played a series in Colorado. I remember the whole family was there," recalled Tankersley. "I wasn't nervous myself. It was pretty exciting. For my family, that was a different story—for my dad especially. He was nervous for the both of us."

◆ MARK TEIXEIRA ◆

Once in awhile you come across a kid who seems destined to be a major leaguer. Mark Teixeira was one of those kids. His baseball-loving family dressed him in a baseball uniform and handed him a bat soon after he was born.

"My earliest baseball memory was probably playing Wiffle ball in my backyard," recalled Teixeira. "Wiffle ball was always fun in the backyard. My dad still has pictures and videos of me out there. Nearly from the point I could walk, I had a baseball and a bat in my hand."

A Baltimore, Maryland, native, Teixeira's father, John, was a former Navy pilot, and his son's baseball coach. "My dad wasn't just my coach when I was a kid . . . he was my BEST coach when I was a kid," stated Teixeira. "He taught me how to play the game. I learned basically everything from him when I was a kid. And then, when I got older, he moved into more of an assistant coach role and made sure he was always there and around to help."

The best lesson Teixeira learned from his best coach? "Swing and play hard was the best advice I remember," he said. "When you are out there, make sure you run hard, concentrate on making the right play, and always do your best."

Teixeira went to Mount St. Joseph's High School in Baltimore. In 1997, he was named Maryland's top junior by *USA Baseball*. By the time he was a senior, he had several college offers. He opted for Georgia Tech, with the stipulation that he would turn pro if he was selected early in the June 1998 draft. Because Teixeira's asking price seemed high, many major-league teams passed on him come draft day. It wasn't until the 9th round that the Boston Red Sox took a chance and selected him. But Teixeira could not come to an agreement with the Red Sox, so the big first baseman went off to Georgia Tech.

He had some spectacular years in college and won the Dick Howser Trophy in 2001 as the National Collegiate Baseball Player of the Year. The June draft arrived again, and this time the Texas Rangers selected him in the first round with the 5th overall pick.

A mere two years later, he made his major-league debut, on April 1, 2003, in Angels Stadium in Anaheim. "My family came out to Anaheim to watch me play in my first game," Teixeira recalled. "For me, it was quite a thrill. My dad is my biggest fan—always will be—and he gets a lot of enjoyment watching me play."

Countless All-Star Games, several Silver Sluggers, and multiple Gold Gloves later, Teixeira still turns to his father for direction. "More off the field than on these days," he stated. "I think he got to a point in my career that he really couldn't help me out anymore. He taught me everything he knew. But to his credit, he gave me such a great base of knowledge I was able to be on my own."

◆ JIM THOME ◆

It is said that the best athletes gain success, in part, due to their genes. Jim Thome has some pretty impressive genes . . . and an impressive major-league career. His grandfather Chuck, Uncle Art, and Aunt Caroline were not baseball players, but softball players, and all are in the fast-pitch wing of the Peoria Sports Hall of Fame.

"My father never played professional ball," Thome explained, "but he was very active in baseball and softball. And, we were definitely a baseball family."

Thome's father, Chuck Jr., played softball in the Outlaw League in Peoria, and his two older brothers, Chuck III and Randy, played fast-pitch softball after graduating from Limestone High School.

Jim Thome played baseball—and basketball—in high school. After he graduated in 1988, he went to Illinois Central Junior College, where he again played baseball and basketball. Not surprising, baseball won out. He impressed Cleveland scouts enough to become the Indians' 13th-round pick in the June 1989 draft.

On September 4, 1991, he made his major-league debut in a start at third base against the Minnesota Twins. "My dad was there to see me at my first game. It was in Minnesota. I wasn't so much nervous because I knew he was there. My mom and dad were my biggest fans," said Thome, who singled in his second at-bat for his first major-league hit.

"There are so many things I learned from my dad," the twenty-year major leaguer and five-time All-Star said in retrospect. "You learn integrity from your dad and how to be a man. I learned the importance of family values and how to be a leader from him. I know the kind of role model he was for me and I try to live up to that with my own kids. I learned what he wanted us to do, and no matter what that was, to always work hard at it."

Thome lost his mother in 2005, but remains close to his father. "My dad is one of my best friends. Since the death of my mother, we have only gotten closer."

◆ B. J. UPTON ◆

Melvin Emmanuel Upton picked up a lot from his father—including his nickname. His father was once known as "Bossman," and by association, little Melvin picked up the name, "Bossman Junior." The name stuck and Melvin became B.J. forevermore.

Another thing he picked up from his father was a piece of great advice. "He taught me to always play hard and believe you can do it," recalled Upton. "My dad never let me quit anything. I can remember there were some times when I didn't want to be out there and he always encouraged me to keep going and stay out there. It was a lesson that has gone a long way with me."

Upton looks back fondly on his early days. "My earliest memories were me playing T-ball. Our family still likes looking at those pictures even today!

"My dad was a big Yankees fan and my favorite player growing up was Derek Jeter," Upton continued. "*Now* it's not a big deal, but when I first broke into the big leagues, it was unbelievable to think, 'I'm on the same field as my idol.'"

B.J. and his younger sibling, Justin, made history by becoming the only two brothers in Major League Baseball history to be selected first and second in the first-year player draft. B.J. was the 2nd overall selection (by Tampa Bay) in 2002; his brother was the first player selected in the 2005 draft (by the Arizona Diamondbacks).

Competition is natural between siblings, but since both brothers play in the majors, does dad have a favorite? "I would like to say it's me," laughed B. J. Upton, "but I think it's pretty equal. Mom always took care of my little brother, so if I had to guess who my dad's favorite would be, it's probably me."

Although Upton has now established himself as a successful major-league player, he still turns to his father for advice. "I would hope everyone would always turn first to their father for advice," Upton passionately stated. "He has always been there for me and hopefully always will be."

◆ JUSTIN UPTON ◆

The Upton family is working on leaving its mark on Major League Baseball. B.J. and Justin Upton are already the first brother combination to be selected as the No. 1 and No. 2 draft choices in different years (B.J. as the 2nd overall pick in 2002; Justin as the first overall pick in 2005). But it all started with their father, Manny.

"He told us, no matter what you are doing, there is always someone that is working a little harder than you are and trying to get better than you are," said Justin Upton. "Whether it is in sports or academics, you can't stop working because there is always someone working just a little harder and longer than you. There is always someone knocking at your door to pass you."

Justin said he was the one trying to catch up to B.J. in his younger days. "My earliest baseball memory was watching my brother playing T-ball and I was always tagging along. I wasn't quite old enough to play. My dad was coaching B.J. at the time and I was always there with them trying to be a part of the team. I didn't necessarily get to play, but I felt like I was part of something with my brother playing and my dad being the coach. I did what little brothers do . . . I tagged along."

When Upton got old enough to play, his father had to conquer the challenge of how to split his time between two blooming athletes. "He coached me here and there," said Upton. "In fact, I met my very best friend in the world when I was six years old and his dad was the head coach. But my dad would help out as an assistant coach because he had to split time with me and B.J. Also, B.J. was getting into the higher levels and my dad wanted to be there, but he still found time to coach me. He was splitting time between the two of us, but I spent a lot of time with him also."

Upton said he relishes all the time he did get with his father and brother as a child. "Anytime we were at a baseball tournament or on the field or traveling it was so much fun and that is what I will always remember as a kid. Getting the opportunity to play baseball, being with my brother and dad are the things I will always remember because I was doing what I loved and that was playing baseball. I remember each fall going from football games to baseball games and having to pull over on the side of the road and changing our football gear and putting on the baseball uniform so I could get dressed from one sport to another. The only thing that was the same was the cleats. It was part of the grind we did as kids . . . but I loved every minute of it."

The passion for the game of baseball is a family trait, according to Upton. "Baseball has always been my dad's love since he was a kid, too. That is always what he wanted us to play," said Upton. "He never told us to play the game or to be baseball players. He always left that up to us, but baseball was always his first love."

Being the younger brother had its advantages, according to Upton. "I never thought about it growing up as a competition. But the two of us were always very competitive," said Upton. "Whenever we were playing in the yard, or down the street or wherever we played, we were competitive. Maybe there wasn't so much competition because B.J. was so much older. He was three years older and in baseball terms that is a long time when you are younger. But he being older made me a better baseball player. I was able to watch B.J.'s progression as a player and that made me push a little bit harder so I could get to his level."

Who does Justin think is his dad's favorite between his two competitive sons? "I would have to say it is B.J.," he stated. "He is Junior and he is the namesake of my father," admitted Justin. "But my mom's favorite will always be me!"

The youngest Upton graduated from Great Bridge High School in Virginia in 2005, then was selected by the Arizona Diamondbacks as the very first pick of the June draft. A short time later the outfielder made his major-league debut—on August 2, 2007, in San Diego. And the major-league legacy of the Upton brothers began.

"The biggest challenge for me is the mental side of the game . . . staying confident and believing in your abilities," confessed Upton. "Sometimes talent makes you lose sight as to why you are in the big leagues. When you lose sight of what you have, the best thing to do is to revert back to being natural and playing the game like your dad taught you to play it."

He said his dad is still there to support him. "Even to this day I turn to him for advice," revealed Upton. "I've had three batting coaches here in Arizona and still none of them know my swing as well as my dad. It's no disrespect to them—I trust these coaches. But at the same time my dad watches every single game, he watches every single swing, and he knows what's going on and, when something is not right, he is there for me."

B.J. (left) and Justin (right) Upton

◆ ANDY VAN SLYKE ◆

Many successful major league players had their fathers as their coaches . . . but as their school principals, too? Andy Van Slyke had to deal with that as well as the normal pressures of being a teenager.

"My dad was actually a great influence," Van Slyke shared, "in a sense because he wasn't overbearing. He never said, 'You had a bad game,' no matter what sport I played or how I played. In my dad's book, I always had a good game. He was always positive. My dad was also my principal from grades seventh through ninth, and then he switched schools when I went to senior high and was my principal there until I graduated."

With your father watching over you nearly every minute of every day, the pressure could become unbearable. But Van Slyke turned it into a positive.

"My dad was a baseball man and he was a heck of a pitcher," said Van Slyke. "But I think the greatest lesson he taught me was the lesson of how people perceive you. Because I was the principal's son, too, there was an understanding that you always had a responsibility to being in that situation whether it was at school or in the field."

The responsibility Van Slyke shouldered paid off in the long run, as he became the first-round selection of the St. Louis Cardinals (and 6th overall pick) in the June 1979 draft. He went on to become a five-time Gold Glove winner and a three-time All-Star who was renowned for his wit as his defense during his thirteen-year major-league career.

He made his MLB debut on June 17, 1983, but as Van Slyke recollected memories of his father, his thoughts turned to his own sons. "I'm sure he was there. I know I have two boys in the game myself, so their first game in the big leagues will mean more to me than my first game."

Van Slyke is the father of four boys—AJ, Scott, Jared, and Nathan. AJ and Scott were selected in the 2005 draft—Scott, out of high school in the 14th round by the Los Angeles Dodgers; AJ out of the University of Kansas in the 23rd round by the St. Louis Cardinals.

◆ JUSTIN VERLANDER ◆

"I was nine years old and I got the chance to pitch for the first time in Little League. For me, that was my first memory of the game," recalled the 2006 American League Rookie of the Year, 2011 Most Valuable Player (MVP), and Cy Young Award winner, Justin Verlander.

"My father was my coach in Little League and when he wasn't the coach, he was always involved. He did what dads do," Verlander stated. Then he added with a smile, "He probably wanted to watch me to make sure I wasn't doing anything wrong!"

According to Verlander, the 2nd overall selection in the Major League Baseball June draft in 2004, his father, Richard, gave him the push he needed to succeed. "Without him, and him motivating me, I wouldn't be where I am today. When you grow up and are on your own, it's all about self-motivation. And to go the places you want to go, you have to be able to work hard.

"My dad was a motivator for me. I have a little brother who was a self-motivator," said Verlander of his brother, Ben, who was selected by the Detroit Tigers in the June 2010 draft. "When I was little I did not have the ability to motivate myself. My dad gave me the boost I needed."

His father was not in attendance for his no-hitter on June 12, 2007 (although he followed it on pins and needles from home in Virginia). But he was in attendance for another big moment— his son's major-league debut on July 4, 2005, in Cleveland.

"It was something special to have my family watch," Verlander reminisced. "It was not just my first time in the big leagues, which makes it all the more exciting, but to have my family share it with me made it a special moment and time for me."

With so much success in the world of baseball, memories of
his early days would surely include something like his first
no-hitter, thrown in middle school, but this likable right-
hander—who can reach 100 mph on the radar gun with
regularity—remembers something else, "I always wanted to
know where I got my athletic ability from," he grinned.

"By the time I turned ten years old I could throw a ball further than my dad," he recalled. "It was at this point my father
knew he had to get some special coaching for me . . . but he was
always there for the love."

♦ TIM WAKEFIELD ♦

Tim Wakefield has had a very successful career in the major leagues, thanks to his knuckleball and his father.

Wakefield's father was his coach in Little League until he was twelve years old. The father and son would play catch in the evening. "We'd throw for awhile, and then he'd start to get tired," recalled the quiet right-hander. "He'd throw the knuckleball so that I would miss it and then have to go run after it. It was a way of making me tired so he could go in and get dinner."

It was also a pitch he would always remember. "As a kid, I always had it in my back pocket," Wakefield recalled.

The winner of the prestigious Roberto Clemente Award in 2010, Wakefield has been playing in the majors for over nineteen years. But his first baseball memory dates back to his T-ball days. "I remember I was five years old and playing T-ball. I just remember how much fun I had putting on the uniform, the cap, and going to play."

Wakefield graduated from Eau Gallie High School in Melbourne, Florida. He then attended Florida Tech, also in Melbourne, where he was the team MVP as their first baseman in his sophomore and junior years, while setting a school record with 40 career home runs.

The Pittsburgh Pirates selected him in the 8th round of the June 1988 draft as a first baseman. But his first professional season did not go very well. "I think they first saw me throw the knuckleball while I was goofing off in the outfield," speculated Wakefield. "They asked if I could throw that thing for a strike. I said I suppose I could." By 1990, he had been converted to a pitcher.

On July 31, 1992, his dream became a reality when he made his major-league debut against the St. Louis Cardinals. "My father was there," Wakefield recalled. "It was my debut and he got the opportunity to be there and I was very nervous he was there, but I am glad he was there." So glad, that Wakefield ended up throwing a complete game victory.

"The biggest thing I remember my father telling me was, 'When things get tough that is the time to bow your neck'— which means get your head down and don't quit," Wakefield explained of the piece of fatherly advice that helped him get to, and stay in, the majors. "Stick it right to them."

◆ MATT WIETERS ◆

South Carolina native Matt Wieters has not been in the majors long, but he has certainly made an impact and his father deserves much of the credit.

"My dad coached me all the way from Little League through high school. I played for a different coach when I hit high school," said Wieters, "but I still played summer ball and that is where my dad continued to coach me. We spent a lot of time together as coach and player."

He continued, "We spent a lot of time practicing and playing down at the Little League field near our house. It was this little sandlot field and I can remember all of the good times my dad and I had there—playing catch, him coaching, him throwing batting practice to me, and doing what kids love to do. It was the whole experience I remember. Just being around my dad was the important thing for me. It was good times we shared. He was always a big baseball guy and it makes me feel so proud that I have been able to make it so far in this game and having him with me for my entire journey. It makes him proud, too, after all the hard work we put in this game, it was able to pay off."

Wieters graduated from Stratford High School, and then went on to Georgia Tech, where the multitalented catcher became one of just three players in Georgia Tech history to earn All-American honors on two occasions.

The Baltimore Orioles selected him with their first pick of the June 2007 draft (5th overall). He made his major-league debut less than two years later, on May 29, 2009, against the Detroit Tigers. And, just about two years after that, the six foot five catcher was named to his first All-Star team.

"My dad watches my games all of the time," Wieters shared. "He goes to as many games as possible. Whenever I am struggling or if I want a different point of view, I'll turn to him. He is there when I need him and when I need the advice. He is my eyes in the sky!"

Looking back on what his father taught him through the years, Wieters said, "The greatest lesson my dad taught me goes with the greatest lesson one learns in life. My dad always taught me to play hard, but remember to have fun. He would always say, 'Go to practice, play hard, work hard, and all the time have fun.' I couldn't wait for my dad to come home every night so we could throw in the backyard. Baseball was always something we had in common and we always loved doing things together. One of his catchphrases was 'have fun'; it was the most important advice he ever gave me."

◆ TY WIGGINTON ◆

"My dad was my coach beginning in Little League and then all the way up to junior varsity," said Ty Wigginton, a major-league utility player since 2002. "He then went on to be an assistant coach during my senior year in high school."

Wigginton grew up in San Diego, California, and was a Padres season ticket holder. "One of my first baseball memories growing up was going with my dad to a lot of Padres games and watching players like Tony Gwynn, Joe Carter, Gary Sheffield, and all of those guys."

After graduating from Chula Vista High School in 1995, he went to the University of North Carolina, Asheville. Following his junior year, Wigginton was selected by the New York Mets in the 17th round of the June 1998 draft. With his 2002 major-league debut, he became the first baseball player from UNC-Asheville to make it to the majors.

"I was with the New York Mets when I first got called up," recalled Wigginton. "We were playing in Los Angeles, so my parents drove up to see me play against the Dodgers." Wigginton did not appear in that series, but he did make his debut in the next series, on May 16 in San Diego. "They then went back to San Diego for a series," he continued. "I know it was fun for them. He was so proud to see me play on the field where the two of us saw so many games in the past. My dad has helped me to live my dream."

Wigginton has played for seven different major-league teams, but still stays in touch with his father. "I'll call him up and ask him what he thinks about a lot of different things," he said. "We talk baseball all the time and he still keeps himself busy with the game coaching a little high school baseball."

Wigginton took a moment to summarize what his father has meant to him in his career. "I think the greatest lesson I learned from my dad was probably the work ethic," he said. "On the baseball side, he taught me to have a love for the game. He always had a love for the game and he passed this on to me."

◆ BERNIE WILLIAMS ◆

This book is a celebration of the relationships between fathers and their sons. But to Bernie Williams, recalling memories of his father soon after his passing, it is also a tribute to a man he greatly loved and admired.

"From the point I joined organized ball he was instrumental in my career," said Williams. "He taught me the game at a very young age. When I was eight years old, he used to take me and my brother every day after school to the Little League stadium and either play catch, hit us fly balls, or throw us pitches to hit. He was so patient."

The All-Star outfielder recalled that his father "used to be pretty strict and wanted us to work hard, but at the same time he wanted us to have fun. It was a rare quality because if it's not fun, then it's not worth playing."

The fifteen-plus-year major leaguer shared the greatest advice he received from his father: "Pursue excellence, be persistent, work hard, and lay off the high ones."

Williams said his father remained his hitting coach, even after he'd been in the big leagues for a decade. "He used to volunteer advice whether I wanted it or not," Williams recalled with a smile.

A five-time All-Star and four-time World Series champion, Williams has had much success in his life, not only in baseball, but as a classical and jazz guitarist. "I owe my dad everything that I have become. I am who I am because of him," an emotional Williams said.

Williams said he admired many people while growing up, but none more than his father. "I used to watch a lot of players, like Rickey Henderson and Dave Winfield," said Williams, "but my hero was my dad, bar none, no question about it. He was my hero."

♦ RANDY WINN ♦

Nice guys do not always finish last . . . just ask Randy Winn.

He grew up with strong, supportive, and involved parents. "My first baseball memory was probably playing out in the backyard with the Wiffle-ball bat," said Winn, "and I also remember swinging that big chunky bat with my little hat on. I remember how my father would always play out there with me."

His father not only played with him in the backyard, he became his coach. "My father was my coach in Little League, from age six on up. He has always been my coach, just like he has always been my dad," said the outfielder.

"My father was always there supporting me, saying things like, 'Don't give up!' or 'Don't forget to practice.'"

Winn went to Ramon Valley High School where he excelled in baseball and basketball. He went on to Santa Clara University, where he continued his exploits in the two sports.

The six foot two athlete caught the eye of the Florida Marlins, who selected him in the 3rd round of the June 1995 draft. In 1997, Winn was selected by the Tampa Bay Devil Rays in the expansion draft.

His major-league dream came true the following year when he made his debut as a pinch runner on May 11, 1998, against the Cleveland Indians. His parents did not see him in Florida however. "Their first game was in Seattle and I faced Randy Johnson," recalled Winn of the May 24 contest.

"I got called up and it was during a road trip and because another player went on the disabled list, I then got my chance. But I was always thinking back then that this was going to be a short trip up for a short period of time. I'm from Oakland," explained Winn, "so we were going to Seattle and then Oakland, and I thought I was going to be sent down again. My parents came up to see me in Seattle to make sure they had a chance to see me play. Fortunately for me, I ended up staying on the team and the other guy never made it off the disabled list. So they got to see me up in Seattle and then at home in Oakland."

The thirteen-year major leaguer said his parents have helped him keep his playing career in perspective. "They are very proud, but they are also very quiet and private," Winn shared. "I think they would rather hear that I am a nice person than a great baseball player. It has always been more important for them what I do off the field than on the field. I think my mom likes hearing the good stories about me more than anything else. Especially when somebody in the area or someone they know tells her, 'Your son is so nice! He signed this ball for my son and he didn't even know that I knew you (meaning my mom).' I really think that warms her heart."

◆   RANDY WOLF   ◆

Randy Wolf grew up outside of Los Angeles knowing he wanted to be a baseball player. "Probably as early as six years old I wanted to be a baseball player and I always wanted to pitch," stated Wolf. "Even though I played every sport, I just didn't get excited about the rest like I did for baseball. I remember watching *This Week in Baseball* with Mel Allen every Saturday morning. I remember watching every Sunday Dodgers game listening to Vin Scully. It was something about the game. Even today, I watch football but I just don't get into it. I didn't have the love of the game except for baseball."

The left-hander was coached by his father in Pony League. "My father taught me the principles of baseball, but the greatest lesson he taught we both learned together," said Wolf. "When I was a kid I had the most horrible temper in the world. My dad was a pretty intense guy as well. When the two of us got together, we seemed to constantly butt heads. We were good for each other."

Wolf said his older brother, Jim, also had a big impact on his development. "I greatly admired my dad growing up, but I also admired my brother," said Wolf. "My brother was seven years older than me and I always tried to compete and be better than him. I remember when he was fifteen and I was eight we had a race. I couldn't understand why he beat me. It didn't make any sense to me why he would have won. This competition helped me as the years went on. It wasn't a bad competition, but I always tried to get to his level."

That brother, Jim Wolf, ended up in the major leagues as well, working as an umpire.

Randy Wolf attended Pepperdine University and was selected by the Philadelphia Phillies in the 2nd round of the June 1997 draft. The All-Star has played with the Phillies, his hometown Los Angeles Dodgers, and the Milwaukee Brewers. But his father never got to see him pitch in the majors.

"He passed away in my senior year of high school," said Wolf, "but I still feel his presence and that he is still looking down at me. Who knows what it is, but I still feel like there is a connection to him. I know he is looking down and is proud."

◆ JASON WOOD ◆

California native Jason Wood got to the majors thanks to his father, a lot of hard work, and practice, practice, practice.

"My dad was always my coach," said Wood. "He was the one who got me going in this game. He was always in the field standing back and watching over everything. He was obviously the person who taught me the game.

"I will never forget the times we'd go," recalled Wood of the Saturday mornings when his father wasn't working, "to Fresno State University and use their batting cages before the team would get there. He would throw and throw and throw, pitch after pitch to me. Then he'd take me back to my own game later that day. During the week, he'd do the same thing. We spent a lot of time together just in the batting cages. If they weren't open, then we'd go to the softball cages. My dad would always find a way to get it done."

Wood's father had more advice for his son. "It wasn't about baseball, but rather how to be a good person in life and to always do the right thing," shared Wood. "That is what he always instilled in me and now I get to carry this on with my own teammates and especially with my family. My dad always loved for me to play in the game, but he always wanted me to have fun with it."

His father was not at his debut, but he was there for an equally memorable game. "I will never forget it," Wood remembered enthusiastically. "My dad was there for my first major-league home run. It was at Fenway Park in September 1998. It was unbelievable and he was there for it!"

Many baseball players are superstitious, although many won't admit to it. "Funny thing, my *dad* was superstitious," said Wood. "If I went hitless, he wouldn't stay in the same spot very long—he would move around the ballpark to a different spot. If I did get a couple of hits, he would stay in that spot for the remainder of the game. I guess you can call him a floater! He is still one today."

Wood said his father's role in his life has evolved from baseball coach to a kind of life coach. "My relationship with my dad is on a different level now," Wood revealed. "I've got coaches now that I'm able to turn to for their advice concerning the game. Other advice and questions about life, I still turn to my dad for advice."

◆ DAVID WRIGHT ◆

David Wright's father was similar to many fathers excited to have a son and eager to teach him how to play ball. "I can remember when I was real, real young my father and my grand-father were teaching me about baseball," recalled Wright. "They taught me to hit with the Wiffle bat and ball in my grandfather's backyard. They are my earliest memories of baseball."

It didn't stop there, as his father continued to teach him as he grew. "My dad was my coach early on, in T-ball and then in my first few years in Little League," said Wright. "I remember my dad used to take me into the outfield and work with me all the time. He was a good batting coach, but," he added with a big grin, "he is very comfortable letting the professionals teach me now."

One of his father's best habits was always being there for his son. "I know my dad didn't miss any of my games growing up, through Little League and high school," Wright reminisced. "I can remember my grandfather being with him all the time as well. It was tremendous having that kind of support. He was never the type of dad that yelled from the dugout or stands, but rather you'd find him in the corner eating sunflower seeds and soaking it all up. He never yelled at an umpire. My dad was always quiet. He was silent and supportive, but he is still the first one I go to if I have any kind of problem or need help or just advice. I just give him a call and he's always there to answer."

Wright was selected by the New York Mets in the supple-mental round (following the first round and prior to the second) of the June 2001 draft out of Hickory High School in Chesapeake, Virginia. He made his major-league debut just a few years later, at the age of twenty-one. His early success was a credit to his unmatched work ethic.

The All-Star third baseman also credits his father for helping him become the successful player he is today. "Even to this day, my dad is a calming influence in my life," said Wright. "He taught me at a very young age not to hang my head and dwell on my failures. He would never get angry at me for struggling or making an error. He would get upset with me if I struck out and then came back to the dugout hanging my head in disap-pointment and not rooting for my teammates. It was a great lesson to learn. Even to this day, I tend to take slumps home with me. Today, my dad is my best mental and emotional coach. If I get into a bad mood, he's the first person I turn to—to help brighten me up and get me to think positively again."

Wright reminisced about his youth a little more. "My dad used to take me to the elementary school or the field every day or every other day and throw me batting practice, shag fly balls, and hit me grounders. He actually blew out his rotator cuff when I was younger after throwing me batting practice one day.

"It was the dedication he used to show me," Wright recalled thoughtfully. "After working all day—and instead of going home and either relaxing or doing something for him—he would grab the bucket of balls, and me and my brother were off to the fields. Ultimately, he knew I loved the game and that was enough for him."

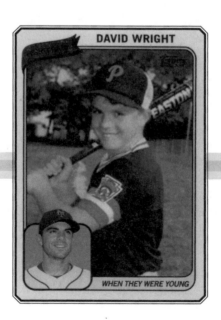

◆ JAMEY WRIGHT ◆

Jamey Wright was coached by his father when he was young. "He wasn't necessarily the head coach all the time," clarified Wright, "but he was still a coach and he was always there doing a little of everything. He might even have been my best coach. He knows me better than anyone."

Wright said that he needed a push from his dad just to get interested in the game of baseball. "I remember I was five years old and I was going to my first T-ball game with my dad. I was more into playing in the dirt. And then by the second year I realized I could actually hit and catch the ball," recalled Wright. "It was at that point I started to get interested in the game. It also got pretty fun for me at the same time. I grew up to love the game early on."

Love for the game was apparent in the six foot six right-handed pitcher when he graduated from Westmoore High School in Oklahoma and then was selected by the Colorado Rockies in the first round (28th overall) of the 1993 draft.

Wright credited his father with investing him, not only with a love for the game, but the proper attitude to succeed in baseball. "The best lesson my dad taught me was to keep everything positive. He taught me to look at the positive in all that I do. Don't take it too hard. Don't let it get you down. Don't get too high or too low. That is what he has always taught me," Wright said emphatically. "Just when you think you are the worst player ever that has played this game and you're struggling, he is always there to point out the positive and remind me of the good things that have happened. Whenever you are going great he is always there to let you know to not let it get to your head."

Wright quickly went through the minor-league system and got the call to the majors on July 3, 1996. "My first game in the major leagues was in San Francisco and my parents both flew out there to watch me pitch," Wright recalled. "I remember I had about twenty people that made the game—for whatever reason there was a bunch of cheap flights from Oklahoma to California. It was funny. I remember they were all wearing shorts and a T-shirt thinking it was summer, but it was San Francisco and by the end of the game they all had bought Giants sweatshirts to keep warm, even though I was with the Colorado Rockies and they were wearing the wrong team logo."

The nineteen-year pro continues to take advice from his dad. "My dad is always the person that is quick to throw out suggestions just when I need them. He has watched me play and has taught me the game since day one," said Wright, who also credits his mother with helping him succeed.

"My parents have always been supportive. They have always been there for me with whatever I need. I always know that I can turn to them . . . and my dad continues to be my best friend."

◆ JARET WRIGHT ◆

"Like father, like son" is a common phrase used when boys imitate their fathers. Jaret Wright not only imitated his father, he followed in his footsteps.

Clyde "Skeeter" Wright, Jaret's father, was a major-league starting pitcher for ten years in the 1960s and 1970s. Jaret was also a starting pitcher in the majors for ten years. But he said it all started when he was a kid.

"My dad was kind of my honorary coach in Little League," said Jaret Wright. "He didn't want to step on any toes having been in the game since I was a little kid. I remember him stepping down when I hit high school, leaving the job then to my other coaches. He's also had a pitching school that he's run since I was little as well."

Strangely enough, Jaret's most vivid baseball memory growing up didn't have anything to do with his father and his professional career. "I remember once, when I was seven or eight years old, I took a line drive to the chest," recalled Jaret. "I went right down to the ground and my dad came up to me and said, 'Well, it will feel better once it stops hurting.' Then he told me to get up . . . and so I got back up and went back to play."

Having a father who was in the majors, surely Jaret had the edge on other players? Not necessarily. "He's your dad first," explained the six foot two right-hander, "and for any son growing up, it's sometimes difficult listening to the words of your father. Then you grow up and move out on your own. Then you begin to listen a little more. As the years passed, I think our relationship has only gotten better."

Jaret graduated from Katella High School in Anaheim, California, in 1994. The Cleveland Indians selected him in the first round (10th overall) of the June draft that year. Three years later, he found himself in the same situation his father had faced thirty-one years before—making his major-league debut. "It was in June 1997, against the Twins," Jaret shared. "Ironically, we both had our first starts against Minnesota. I remember my dad said to me that day how it was so much easier to pitch in his first game than to watch me play in my first game."

Like father, like son, both of the Wrights won their debuts.

But it wasn't always so easy for the younger Wright. "When I'd struggle early on I'd call my dad and ask him what he saw in the way I was pitching and ask his advice," said Jaret.

"I do think the biggest thing is that you've got to know yourself really well," he continued, "because in this game you move around a lot and you end up experiencing a lot of different coaches. You've got to know yourself and then you can eventually establish checkpoints along the way that then help you know what to look for. That is why my dad is so important to me."

◆ MICHAEL YOUNG ◆

"My dad was my coach all through Little League until I was about fourteen years old," said Michael Young, a DH/infielder for the Texas Rangers and seven-time All-Star.

"I was about eight or nine years old the first year he coached me," recalled Young. "I remember I made an out and then came back into the dugout. I slammed my helmet. I threw my bat. My dad just looked at me. At that point, I knew it wasn't the right thing to do. From that point on, I knew this game wasn't about being perfect and my focus was on the next at-bat and on the next play. Every now and again when I want to cut loose a little, I think back to that moment and what my dad taught me about how important it was to keep your emotions inside."

Young credits his father with helping him develop his self-esteem, as well as his emotional discipline and baseball skills. "My dad was great," Young said. "He was always committed to the fact that I loved baseball, so he was always supportive. My dad always made me feel that I was worthwhile. He always wanted me to have fun. And, it was because of him that I love baseball so much."

Young was drafted in 1994—out of Bishop Amat High School in La Puente, California—by the Baltimore Orioles, but he did not sign. He instead went to the University of California, Santa Barbara, and was selected again, this time by the Toronto Blue Jays, in the 5th round of the June 1997 draft. He quickly rose through the minor leagues and then, on July 19, 2000, fate stepped in when he was traded to the Texas Rangers, an organization he remains a part of to this day.

"The first game my dad attended was in 2000 when I got called up," Young remembered of his September 29 promotion to the majors. "We were playing in Oakland. In a way, I knew he was proud of me. I'm sure every player will probably tell you the same thing—what they think about the most on that day . . . the people that helped to get them there. My dad is at the top of that list."

The California native appeared in just two games in 2000,

but enjoyed a full season in the majors the following year. "During my rookie year my dad came to see me every game in Texas," recalled Young of his 2001 season. "I remember during one game, it was the bottom of the ninth, there were two outs, and I was up with two strikes. I was pretty nervous. The crowd was on their feet. There must have been forty thousand people standing up and cheering. I knew exactly where the family section was and I looked for him and when I saw him stand up with the rest of the crowd, it felt so good. He was happy and I was happy he was there and then I was able to relax and do what I had to."

Young said he continues to look for his dad at every game he attends. "I step out of the dugout before each game and look for him. I know where he sits, and when I see him I know I can relax."

Young doesn't seek out baseball advice from his father anymore, but "we still talk," he said. "Obviously, I know baseball better than him now. I have been in the big leagues for quite a few years now. But the thing is, he knows me as a person better than anyone and when I need advice for matters off the field, he is there. And, in some cases, [it's] about things that are just as important as the fundamentals and mechanics of the game."

BEN ZOBRIST

Not every future major leaguer comes out of high school or college as a "can't miss" prospect. Ben Zobrist assumed he was more of a "no chance" prospect.

A pitcher and infielder in high school in his native Illinois, Zobrist originally received no major-league or college offers. "When I was done my last high school game," recalled Zobrist, "I was driving around town just thinking, I'm done with baseball for the rest of my life."

His baseball coach coerced him to go to a senior's showcase, where he impressed enough to get a scholarship to Olivet Nazarene University. He transferred to Dallas Baptist University for his senior year. And the unlikely dream came closer to reality when the Houston Astros selected him in the 6th round of the June 2004 draft.

"I remember when I first got drafted," said the switch-hitting infielder. "It was a special time because my dad told me that he had thought back to his own dad, who actually passed away when he was nine years old. If he would have still been around, I know he would have been there and shared in all of my games as I grew up with my dad. It was a special time when I got drafted . . . for all of us."

Zobrist was traded to the Tampa Devil Bay Rays on June 12, 2006, and less than two months later, on August 1, his dream became a reality when he made his major-league debut against Justin Verlander and the Detroit Tigers. "My dad was there for my first game," said Zobrist enthusiastically. "It was great! It was a thrill running on the field. I remember meeting up with my parents after the game. We talked about the game and I could tell my father was so proud."

It stirred memories for Zobrist of his baseball passion when he was a kid, beginning with his backyard Wiffle-ball field. "It was always a special thing for me and my brothers when we got to play a game of Wiffle ball with my dad," he reminisced. "I still remember how much fun it was for us all. My sister would always be there, too. That's where I learned to switch-hit."

Zobrist now makes his off-season home in Nashville with his wife, Julianna, and son, Zion. But he remains in contact with his father. "I still talk to him about all kinds of things," he said, "but not as much about baseball. When I got to college, he said, 'No more asking me about baseball—you know more than I do now.'"

Still, some of the early lessons about the game and about life that his dad taught Zobrist remain with him.

"My dad was my coach in Little League, and then all the way up until I turned fifteen years old," recalled Zobrist. "Probably the greatest lesson my dad taught me was to work hard. He always told me—if you wanted to be good, then you'll have to work hard and always be prepared to play the game."

MORE ADVICE FOR LITTLE
LEAGUERS AND OTHERS

Just as no two players are the same, no two interviews are the same.

Some players had very limited time, but wanted to share a quick story or lend their advice. A few others had so much to share that some of their advice needed to be emphasized. The result follows—a compilation of quotes meant to pay tribute to fathers, help Little Leaguers, and give advice to any baseball fan.

More pearls of wisdom from those who have lived through it all . . .

My dad never really pushed me. He wanted me to have fun and to enjoy the game. He didn't worry too much about instruction, he just wanted me to enjoy baseball for what it is and figured the rest would take care of itself.

—GARRETT ANDERSON

My dad taught me most of what I know about baseball. He was my coach and I will always be his son. I learned everything from my dad. I learned about baseball and what it meant to be a good person. I have always asked him for advice and I still do today. There is always something he has to tell me. When it comes to baseball my dad has always been able to tell me when I am doing something wrong. I love my dad and I am proud to be his son.

—MIGUEL CABRERA

If I was in a slump I would call my father, before he passed away. He would be the one telling me, 'You're doing this or you're not doing that.' It was those little details that would help me do better in this game.

—ORLANDO CABRERA

Go out and have fun. That is some-thing I always did and that is what I continue to do. If you can learn it when you're young then hopefully it can stay with you all your life. Unfortunately, at this level of play we have to face a lot of different challenges but I still try to remember those lessons I learned in Little League.

—JOHNNY DAMON

My dad always taught me to work hard. Working hard was always the most important thing to my dad. And that is the lesson I will always remember from him.

—JEFF DAVANON

Keep playing . . . just have fun no matter how bad you might think things are going.

—WADE DAVIS

You learn so many lessons from your dad as you grow up, I can't pick the greatest one. I still turn to my father for advice once in awhile; although sometimes the tide changes and it turns out I'm giving the advice to him. Today we talk more like friends and not as much like father and son anymore. I have my own family and kids. Life has given me a new expe-rience and I'm the father now.

—JIM EDMONDS

My advice for Little Leaguers outside of the generic "have fun" or "work at it" came directly from my father. My dad would always stress to me about the importance of hustle. His reason being that it is the one thing you can always control. There are so many uncontrollable factors that go on in this game, but hustle never goes in a slump. It's the greatest way to get noticed; it's a great way to overachieve and open eyes no matter what level you're at.

—SAM FULD

My dad was always good at encouraging me. He was good at saying things like, "Don't give up." His favorite expression has always been, "Don't give them a reason!" My mother has always been good at giving a lot of mental advice. What I will always be thankful for is that my parents have always believed in me and they continue to help me out even today.

—LEE GARDNER

My dad always taught me to work hard, a lot of hard work. It was a big part of my life and our family. He never missed a game. All I ever wanted to be, even when I was a kid, was a ballplayer. I loved every minute of it and it has been the dream that I was able to chase.

—JASON GIAMBI

Just go out and have fun. The difference today with Little League is that the coaches seem to be a lot more competitive and way too intense. Just remember to go out and learn the game right, play with your buddies, and, again, have fun!

—JACK HANNAHAN

Have fun. That is the biggest thing to remember. You always have to have fun playing the game. I think too many people pay so much attention nowadays to winning and losing and all sorts of things and yet the only thing they should be worrying about is having fun. I still remember my Little League days and the fun I had. Those days were a long time ago, but I remember them fondly.

—DEREK JETER

In my short career so far, the greatest part of being a major leaguer is being able to play against the greatest players in the world.

—DUSTIN MCGOWAN

My dad basically taught me how to play the game from Little League on up. He taught me everything I know. My dad helped to make me the person I am.

—BRETT MYERS

Have fun! That is the biggest thing you have to remember when you are a kid. It's also the biggest thing for us here, too, even at this level. It's all about the fun you are having. Always remember the fun times, like playing on the grass. Whenever we get away from Tropicana Field and get off this Astroturf and get the opportunity to play on real grass and dirt, I know every ballplayer remembers and enjoys that type of experience. All of those outdoor smells help to remind us what the game was all about when we were kids. It's what it's all about!

—DAVID PRICE

My dad would always say, "Hit the ball right back where it came from"—meaning he always taught me to hit the ball right back up the middle when I was a little kid. It was one of those things that he taught me that I still use today, and, as a major leaguer, it is still important today.

—REED JOHNSON

My dad taught me to always play the game the right way. He taught me to play hard and have dedication to whatever I am doing.

—AARON ROWAND

"There is a lot of emphasis put on instruction and competition at the little league level. I would like the focus to shift toward developing a love for the game and really having as much FUN as possible. Having fun and loving the game should always be the number one priority. Learning techniques and getting the competitive edge will be easier and almost natural when fun and the love of the game are at the forefront."

—CARLOS PENA

Have fun . . . play the game the right way and no matter what you do when you are in between the lines, just enjoy it. It's a lot of fun and you never know when your last day is going to be.

—JUSTIN RUGGIANO

My dad bought me my first glove. I remember it said "Mike Schmidt" so I thought that was pretty cool. I was seven or eight years old. I remember throwing rocks but I never had my own glove until then. I had always wanted to play baseball. He bought me the glove and then taught me how to have a catch. I will never forget that day!

—JASON SCHMIDT

Always remember that this is the greatest time in baseball. Just go out there and have some fun and enjoy your lives. There is no reason to feel or place any pressure on yourself. Have some fun and enjoy the game in Little League—that is when it is fun. You get to run around, get dirty, and get pizza, visit the snack bar or have a Happy Meal after the game or whatever. We used to go to Shakey's Pizza Parlor when I was younger. When we got there it was all about the pizza and playing pinball or video games and seeing who could get the highest score. As soon as the game was over, all I cared about was the pizza.

—JAMES SHIELDS

Have fun playing. When you are a kid the game is so much fun. I'm in the big leagues now and I know it is a totally different outlook for me, but for kids it should still be about fun. Putting on the uniform and spikes and playing on Saturday and just having fun out there. It wasn't about winning or losing. You didn't worry about anything but just playing. So again, the best advice I have for Little Leaguers is to have fun and never lose sight of that.

—SHANNON STEWART

FIELD OF DREAMS

"If you build it, he will come."

Any baseball fan worth his weight can tell you that quote came from the movie *Field of Dreams*. The line was voted as one of top forty movie quotes of all time by the American Film Institute.

But that is not the quote that resonates with fans of the movie, bringing lumps in the throat and tears to the eyes. "Hey Dad, wanna have a catch?" gets that honor. Strangely enough, however, that was not the way the line was originally written. Director Phil Alden Robinson explained, "In the script I felt it was important for the father and son to understand who each other was, but not to say it out loud. (It was sort of the equivalent of Doc not being able to step across the foul line and leave the field.) We shot and cut the scene in a way that I thought made absolutely clear that each character knew who the other was through looks and other nonverbal means. But when we had our first test screening, the audience told us they felt it was unfair for Kevin to know the catcher was his father, and not tell him. They just didn't see what I was hoping they'd see—that the father knew. So we changed the line from 'Hey, you wanna have a catch?' to 'Hey Dad, you wanna have a catch?' And at the next screening, the scores went way up. Go figure."

Robinson himself played catch with his father. "I played catch with my dad quite a lot—it's one of my favorite childhood memories—but he was never a coach."

Major League Baseball players are not immune to the movie's magic, and that may be why so many of them select *Field of Dreams* as their favorite baseball movie, but Robinson is not sure. "I wonder if it resonates in some way with Roy Campanella's old quote about how you have to be a man to play in the majors, but you also have to have a lot of little boy in you. And I'd guess that most people who made it to the big leagues did spend a lot of time playing catch with their dads at a very young age."

He went on about the movie's success, "I am surprised at the impact the movie has had after all these years when I think of the movie, but not when I think of the book. The Kinsella story still retains a magic for me that no filmmaker can feel for a movie he worked on."

★ ★ ★ ★ ★

"If you build it, he will come."

That famous line was also the inspiration for the famous speech near the end of *Field of Dreams*. But that speech, filled with words that resonate and complete the film, was not written—it was completely ad-libbed by James Earl Jones, who played the character Terence Mann in the movie.

"Neither one of us (himself or Director Phil Alden Robinson) knew how to do that speech," explained Jones. "My wife was convinced it would not be in the movie because it went on for so long. Those kinds of speeches don't end up in movies, but rather on the cutting room floor, because movies are all about image and action. I remember turning to Phil and asking him, 'How do you want to do this?' He said, 'I don't know, how do you want to do this?' I said, 'I don't know' back. 'I can't declaim it, it's not an oration.' Then I said, 'It starts from the child. Let her say the words first, 'They will come, daddy.' I figured my character, Terence Mann, would then pick it up from there. 'They will come . . .' It is simple and from the simple comes the profound and that is what America is all about." (Full speech listed below.)

Jones explained a little about his character in the film. "My character Terence Mann was inspired by the live author J.D. Salinger. In the original novel Salinger is the author sought by the main character. But Phil knew he couldn't use the same real life character for the movie. So he thought, *Who would I like to kidnap?* 'I'd like to kidnap James Earl Jones,' he said with a big laugh. "So that is how I got the role! But what is interesting, the film has never been about color, it is color blind and that is the magic of Phil Robinson's choice."

So are there a lot of similarities between Jones and the fictional author he portrayed? "I'm not a boat rocker or a committed activist like he was," explained Jones. "I was probably more the Terence Man character in his later years. By the end of the film he was much more retrospective and I think of myself much like that in the sense that I think about the words I say. And I certainly wasn't dead! Terence Mann was as dead as the rest, but I didn't know it while we were filming. Phil didn't tell me, but looking back, it was evident in the script. I wouldn't have known how to play the character if I did know. He is a ghost all along. Terence Mann was a ghost and that was born out of the scene when they are in the motel room and the call comes in. They are in mystical territory by this time, that whole world in Minnesota with Old Doc Graham. That is how Doc Graham existed, and how he became a boy again, and how he could grab a hitchhike ride in a van again, and how he could go to the field and walk across those lines again. That is also how Terence Mann could exist too, even though he was a spirit."

Terence Mann was a ghost, meaning "the Ray character was an agent," explained Jones. "Anyone who summons a spirit becomes a channeler or an agent and that was him. His mission though was just to have a catch with his dad. That need manifests itself in many mysterious ways throughout the film. By having this simple catch, it allowed him to have closure with his father."

Jones never had a catch with his father. "I was actually raised by my grandfather and he liked to fish," admitted Jones. "But fishing and having a catch are a lot alike. It's a simple communion that is between two people, nothing needs to be said. It is a ritual that comes of communion. As you toss the ball to one another, you are exchanging images and it is something you share. It is the purest bond that lasts forever. It is generally the first ritual that father and sons share."

Jones believes that so many major leaguers embrace the film "ironically, because it is not just about baseball . . . and their lives (the players) are not just about baseball, but they rarely get a chance to express that," he explained. "Baseball is very different from other sports. Their lives are not about standard heroism. In baseball, every man has a chance to be a hero all on his own. And there is nothing anyone can do to help him. What is amazing about baseball–you have to hit this cylindrical sphere, and the chances of hitting it at all are very rare. The chance of hitting it smack on and sending it some place is almost impossible. It is one of the toughest things anyone can do."

The movie makes many a grown man cry . . . Jones is no exception. "I do cry . . . when the music starts and the catch starts in the backyard."

PHOTO CREDITS

Photos on the following pages appear courtesy of the National Baseball Hall of Fame & Museum: Moises Alou (page 22), Mark Buehrle (page 42), Mike Scioscia (page 200), and Michael Young (page 239).

Photos on the following pages appear courtesy of Dave Schofield: Joba Chamberlain (page 49), Tony Clark (page 50), Coco Crisp (page 53), Michael Cuddyer (page 58), Phil Hughes (page 100), Derek Jeter (page 107), Jeff Francoeur (page 78), Jack Hannahan (page 90), Jeremy Hermida (page 92), Adam Kennedy (page 114), Joe Mauer (page 144), Brian McCann (page 146), Justin Morneau (page 155), Mariano Rivera (page 180/155), Jimmy Rollins (page 194/155), and Bernie Williams (page 227).

Rocco Baldelli (page 25) courtesy of the Baldelli family

Jeff Brantley (page 37) and Jonathan Papelbon (page 163) courtesy of Mississippi State University

Matt Diaz (page 64) and Doug Mientkiewicz (page 149) courtesy of Florida State University

Eric Hinske (page 95) courtesy of University of Arkansas

Trevor Hoffman (page 97) photo by Andy Hayt, courtesy of the San Diego Padres

Matt Joyce (page 112) courtesy of the Joyce family

Brad Lidge (page 127) courtesy of the Lidge family

Evan Longoria (page 132) courtesy of the Longoria family

Mike Lowell (page 137) courtesy of Florida International University

Jake Peavy (page 167) courtesy of the San Diego Padres

Mike Piazza (page 171) photo by Marc Levine courtesy of the New York Mets

David Price (page 246) courtesy of the Price family

Sean Rodriguez (page 188) courtesy of the Rodriguez family

Kenny Rogers (page 191) courtesy of the Rogers family

Scott Rolen (page 193) courtesy of the Rolen family

James Shields (page 203) courtesy of the Shields family

B. J. Upton (page 216) courtesy of the Upton family

Justin Upton (page 219) courtesy of the Upton family

Matt Wieters (page 225) courtesy of Georgia Tech

Ben Zobrist (page 242) courtesy of the Zobrist family

SOURCES

Joba Chamberlain: Yahoo.com, 'Duk, November 5, 2009

Bubba Crosby: ESPN.com, "Flash of Yankee Pride," by Gary Miller

Casey Fossum: Morris News Service, George Watson, March 12, 1999

Sam Fuld: *The Tampa Tribune*, Roger Mooney, April 4, 2011

Derek Jeter: *Westchester Journal News,* Ian O'Connor

Doug Mienkiewicz: *Baseball Digest,* Rick Sorci

Benjie Molina: *New York Times,* Jack Curry, January 29, 2007

Jose Molina: MLB.com, Lyle Spencer, March 21, 2007

Scott Podsednik: *Baseball Digest*, Steve Cline, October 2004

Mariano Rivera: *New York Daily News,* Christian Red, March 13, 2010

Mike Piazza: *Philadelphia Inquirer,* Michael Bamberger, December 27, 1992

Tim Wakefield: *The New York Times,* Joe Sexton, October 9, 1992

Ben Zobrist: *St. Petersburg Times,* Marc Topkin, July 14, 2009